AUTOMOBILES
OF THE
'60s

BY THE AUTO EDITORS OF CONSUMER GUIDE

Publications International, Ltd.

CONTENTS

INTRODUCTION 3

AMC.................4

BUICK 7

CADILLAC 12

CHECKER 16

CHEVROLET 18

CHEVROLET CORVAIR 24

CHEVROLET CORVETTE.................27

CHRYSLER 31

DESOTO 36

DODGE.................38

EDSEL.................43

FORD 44

FORD MUSTANG.................49

FORD THUNDERBIRD 52

IMPERIAL.................55

LINCOLN 59

MERCURY 63

METROPOLITAN.................67

OLDSMOBILE 68

PLYMOUTH.................72

PONTIAC 77

RAMBLER 82

SHELBY.................86

STUDEBAKER 88

PRODUCTION CHARTS.................93

Louis Weber, C.E.O.
Publications International, Ltd.
7373 North Cicero Avenue
Lincolnwood, Illinois 60646

Permission is never granted for commercial purposes.

Manufactured in U.S.A.

8 7 6 5 4 3 2 1

ISBN: 0-7853-3782-2

INTRODUCTION

The symmetry was perfect. It was the Sixties, and just as American society at large was engulfed in violent change, so too did the domestic auto industry hurtle into a turbulent and controversial part of its history.

The horsepower race that had begun in the Fifties accelerated in the Sixties. On top of that, the auto industry expanded its offerings to include a previously unheard-of variety of cars: big personal-luxury hardtops, miserly compacts, potent muscle machines, and sporty pony-cars—something for every taste and budget.

Detroit's marketing language was equally memorable: Wide-Tracks, Scat Packs, Super Sports, and Cobra Jets. All this, plus gasoline that seemed pricey if it topped 30 cents a gallon, combined to make for a unique generation of cars.

Cars of the Sixties were a powerful expression of America's waning postwar euphoria. Here was a decade that produced the Pontiac GTO, a showroom model that could do 0-60 mph about 6 seconds; and the Studebaker Avanti, which crossed the Bonneville Salt Flats at 170 mph. Today, such rowdy performance strikes many as a guilty pleasure, and a mere echo of an era that is long gone. Indeed, by the Seventies a whole host of economic, social, and environmental factors conspired against the flash and dazzle offered by the cars of the Sixties. From cockpit safety to tailpipe emissions—the federal government mandated requirements for those and more.

Ironically, it was the car-buying habits of the public that encouraged the heavy hand of government interference—the same heavy hand that the public soon grew to loathe. Consistently, and to Detroit's undoubted puzzlement, consumers showed themselves unmoved by technical progress and innovation. Consumer apathy caused Chevy's cleverly engineered Corvair to fail in its mission as an economy compact. Buyers yawned at the '61 Pontiac Tempest and its innovative rear transaxle and all-independent suspension; the conventionally engineered Tempest that arrived after 1963 handily outsold the '61. The front-drive '66 Toronado could not match the sales figures of the entirely orthodox Buick Riviera. And Pontiac's economical 1966 overhead-cam six-cylinder engine was almost completely ignored by a public that overwhelmingly preferred gas-guzzling V-8s.

It's significant that most of the decade's technical innovations came from General Motors. Independents like Nash, Hudson, and Packard were gone by 1958, leaving the market to the high-volume Big Three and wobbly American Motors. With its superior size and resources, GM was able to cater to the public's every desire, and win on the changing Sixties playing field. By the end of the decade, a make like Chevrolet, which had basically offered only one kind of car in 1959, was fielding five or six: compacts, sporty compacts, intermediates, standards, luxury, and the occasional sports or "specialty" car. Manufacturing ability of that sort led GM to sales dominance in the Sixties. Ford had successes like the Mustang and Continental Mark III, but these were triumphs of marketing, not technology. In contrast, GM was so big it could just as easily offer radical also-rans like Corvair and Toronado as conventionally engineered winners like Chevy Nova or Olds 88.

Despite GM and Ford's impressive market dominance, a few specialist firms operated profitably in the Sixties by filling small but significant "niche" markets that the giants overlooked or ignored. Carroll Shelby's GT-350 catered to fans of all-out performance, while at the other end of the scale, unglamorous utilitarianism was offered by Checker, which built some 6000 taxicab-tough cars a year.

If the public didn't always respond to sophisticated ideas in the Sixties, it did become more discerning in its overall automotive judgment. Right from 1960, buyers began to reject tailfins, multi-tone paint jobs, pushbutton automatic transmissions, and other frivolities of the Fifties. Seeing that good design now implied something more than five-pound hood ornaments, Detroit responded—and quickly. In fact, the very first Big Three compacts of 1960 not only proved that people still wanted practical cars after a generation of impractical ones, but that Detroit could still build them. The sporty compacts that arrived later in the decade brought home a point long accepted in Europe: One should not opt for the biggest car one can afford, but the best. As a nation of car buyers, we Americans learned a lot in the Sixties.

The uninhibited automotive experimentation of the Sixties is gone, but the cars themselves remain. Forceful, dynamic, and brimming with personality, they are wonderful reminders of a remarkable decade.

1963 Studebaker Avanti sport coupe

1967 Ford Galaxie 500 hardtop coupe

A M C

With its fortuitous late-Fifties emphasis on compact Ramblers, upstart American Motors entered the Sixties a solid fourth in U.S. car sales. By mid-decade, under an optimistic new management team, the firm was boldly challenging the Big Three in nearly every market sector.

Indicative of this expansive new policy was the substitution of AMC for Rambler as the formal name of the marque beginning with the full-size Ambassador and fastback Marlin of 1966. The mid-size Rebel was duly rebadged for '68, when the new Javelin ponycar and two-seat AMX arrived. The Rambler moniker was then phased out entirely after the final, 1969 edition of the '64-vintage American compact [see Rambler].

The '66 AMC Ambassador was a warmed-over version of the reskinned '65 Rambler model, one of the better efforts from the studios of AMC styling vice-president Richard A. Teague. Squarish but clean, it spanned a 116-inch wheelbase, four inches longer than that of the structurally similar 1963-64 design. A new special edition for '66 was the elegantly appointed DPL hardtop coupe, with reclining bucket seats, fold-down center armrests, pile carpeting, and many other standard features.

Ranked below it were sedans, wagons and two-door hardtops in 880 and 990 trim, plus a 990 convertible. All were offered with AMC's veteran 232-cubic-inch "Typhoon" six and optional 287- and 327-cid V8s. Only the top 270-horsepower 327 required premium fuel. Most Ambassadors were ordered with automatic, but a few left the factory with three-speed manual transmission or AMC's novel "Twin-Stick" overdrive. A four-speed synchromesh box was also available for 990s and the DPL.

The big Ambassador evolved nicely through this decade. Wheelbase was stretched two inches for 1967, when new bodyshells with more rounded contours appeared. The convertible became a DPL, only to vanish for '68, a year that saw few other changes of consequence save revised series nomenclature: standard, DPL, and SST. New frontal styling with a more sculpted hood, plastic grille, and horizontal quad headlights marked the '69s, which rode a new 122-inch wheelbase—the longest in AMC history—and boasted standard air conditioning.

AMC's first stab at the booming "personal-car" market uncovered by the Chevy Corvair Monza and Ford's Mustang was the radically styled 1965 Rambler Marlin. Called AMC Marlin for 1966-67, this big fastback hardtop coupe was initially derived from the mid-size 1965-66 Rambler Classic, sharing its 112-inch wheelbase and most front sheetmetal. Teague gave it a rakish roofline with elliptical rear side windows, but the overall effect was clumsy, partly because management raised roof height a critical inch from Teague's original design. The '66 changed only in detail: mildly revised grille, standard front anti-roll bar for six-cylinder models, and newly optional vinyl-roof treatment.

For 1967, the Marlin was fully restyled on that year's longer new Ambassador chassis. Though its roof was virtually unchanged, the extra wheelbase made for a much more handsome car, aided by the same flowing bodylines that were also applied to the Ambassador and Rebel. Mea-

1966 Ambassador convertible

1966 Ambassador hardtop coupe

1967 Ambassador hardtop coupe

1967 Marlin fastback coupe

suring 6.5-inches longer (all of it ahead of the cowl), the '67 was certainly the best-looking of this school—but it was too late. Sales had been low from the start; fewer than 5000 Marlins were built for 1966 and only 2500 for '67. Despite offering the requisite sporty features—optional four-speed manual gearbox, tachometer, bucket seats, and engines with up to 280 bhp—Marlin lacked a sports car's taut, precise handling and manageable size.

Replacing it for 1968 was a far more successful sportster: the Javelin, a semi-fastback hardtop "ponycar" in Mustang's image. Beautifully shaped and exciting, it sold like hotcakes. Over 56,000 were built that first model year, helping AMC out of a four-year sales slump. With standard 232 six, a Javelin cruised at 80 mph; with available 290 V-8, it could do 100 mph. An optional "Go Package" delivered a 343 V-8 with four-barrel carburetor and dual exhausts, plus power front-disc brakes, heavy-duty suspension, and wide tires—good for eight seconds in the 0-60-mph dash and a top end near 120 mph. Fine ride and handling were standard in most any form. On its 109-inch wheelbase, Javelin was longer and thus roomier than the Mustang, Chevrolet Camaro, and Plymouth Barracuda, yet no less dashing.

Javelin remained its shapely self for 1969, as styling predictably changed only in detail. So did options and mechanical components. Base and high-line SST models returned at $2512 and $2633, respectively, but production failed to match the first-year total due to intensified competition, sliding to 40,675.

An exciting mid-1968 newcomer was the AMX, a two-seater created by vertically sectioning the Javelin bodyshell just forward of the C-pillar, resulting in a trim 97-inch wheelbase. With it came a bored-and-stroked 390 V-8 with

forged-steel crankshaft and connecting rods. Also optional for the Javelin, this engine put out a healthy 315 bhp and 425 pounds-feet torque. Standard AMX power was a 225-bhp 290, with Javelin's 280-bhp 343 a step-up option.

Tight suspension, bucket seats, and extra-cost four-speed gearbox made the AMX a capable semi-sports car. Craig Breedlove proved as much by setting 106 new speed

1968 Ambassador SST four-door sedan

1968 Rebel SST convertible coupe

5

1968 Javelin SST fastback coupe

1968 AMX fastback coupe

1968 Rebel SST hardtop coupe

1969 Rebel SST hardtop coupe

1969 Javelin SST fastback coupe

1969 Ambassador SST four-door sedan

records shortly before its introduction. But demand proved much lower than management hoped: 6725 for '68, followed by 8293 of the '69s, which saw little change save for optional availability of "Big Bad" paint colors—a loud blue, orange, and green. After building 4116 of the more serious-looking '70s, the AMX was phased out, though the name itself would resurface periodically in the form of sporty option packages applied to somewhat more mundane AMC products.

As mentioned, Rebels wore AMC badges for 1968, though the basic car had appeared the year before as a Rambler. Replacing the Classic as the firm's intermediate, it rode a 114-inch wheelbase (two inches up on 1963-66) and was available with AMC's usual assortment of sixes and V-8s. The '68 lineup comprised sedans, hardtops, and wagons in 550, 770, and sporty SST trim, while convertibles were offered only in 550 and SST variants. These were AMC's only drop-tops that year and would be the last ever (unless you count the ragtop Renault Alliances offered in the late '80s). Few were built: just 377 and 823, respectively. The '69 line was trimmed to base and SST series. A wider track and a new grille plus a restyled rear deck and taillights were the only changes of note.

In retrospect, AMC's attempt to compete model-for-model with the Big Three was misguided. The AMX and

Javelin were top-flight enthusiast cars, but small size precluded AMC from ever being a serious competitor in the mass market—where the *real* money is—its much more limited resources dictating longer product cycles and fewer interim changes. Worse, the major makes quickly invaded the economy field, Rambler ironically having shown them the way. All this rendered AMC an also-ran by 1970 and contributed heavily to its eventual demise. Nevertheless, the firm gamely managed to hang on all the way through 1987, when America's last independent automaker vanished to become part of Chrysler Corporation.

AMERICAN MOTORS AT A GLANCE, 1966-1969				
	1966	1967	1968	1969
Price Range, $	2404-2968	2519-3143	2443-3245	2484-3998
Weight Range, lbs.	2970-3462	3279-3545	2826-3530	2826-3732
Wheelbases, in.	112-116	118	97-118	97-122
6 Cyl. Engines, hp	145-155	145-155	145-155	145-155
8 Cyl. Engines, hp	198-270	200-280	200-315	200-315

BUICK

The Sixties were highly successful years for Buick, if somewhat less so overall than the Fifties. From about 250,000 cars and ninth place for 1960, the division ended the decade at more than 665,000 units and a tight hold on fifth. By contrast, Buick usually ran fourth or even third in the Fifties.

Still, the make's Sixties performance was impressive. It was owed both to the advent of a smaller companion line, reviving the Special and Skylark names, and to steadily rising demand for big Buicks. On the latter score, consider that only 56,000 top-line Electras were built for 1960, versus nearly 159,000 for '69. During that same time frame, LeSabre production increased from about 152,000 to nearly 198,000. Wildcat, which replaced the mid-range Invicta for '63, began at about 35,000 and finished the decade with almost double that volume. Buick might have fared even better had it not been for the meteoric rise of sister division Pontiac, which took over Buick's traditional place as the nation's top-selling medium-price brand.

Appearing for 1961 was the smallest Buick in half a century, the 112-inch-wheelbase Special. One of the "second-wave" GM compacts following Chevy's Corvair (Oldsmobile's F-85 and Pontiac's Tempest were the others), it initially offered notchback coupe, four-door sedan, and hatchback wagon body styles with choice of base or Deluxe trim at prices spanning a $2300-$2800 range. Power came from a new 215-cubic-inch V-8 with 155 horsepower and, unusual for Detroit, all-aluminum construction. Light, smooth-running, and efficient, it's still in production. (GM later sold manufacturing rights to British Leyland, now Rover Group, which modified it for use in Rover cars and Land Rover utility vehicles beginning in the late Sixties. Today, it also powers the posh Range Rover four-wheel-drive station wagon.)

Responding quickly to the sporty-car craze begun with the 1960 Corvair Monza, Buick fielded a more special Special Deluxe coupe called Skylark as a mid-'61 entry. Bucket seats, deluxe trim, vinyl roof, and a tuned 185-bhp version of the aluminum V-8 helped sell more than 12,000 in its abbreviated debut season. The following year brought Skylark and Special Deluxe convertibles, an optional Borg-Warner four-speed transmission, and sales of more than 153,000 Buick compacts.

Big Buicks changed dramatically in the early part of this decade. The 1960 models—LeSabre, Invicta, Electra, and Electra 225 sedans, station wagons, convertibles, and hardtops—were basically toned-down versions of the wild, all-new '59s. Their 1961 replacements rode identical wheelbases but weighed 100-200 pounds less and looked even cleaner. For 1962, Buick unleashed the Wildcat as a specialty item in the Invicta series. A two-ton, 123-inch-wheelbase luxury hardtop coupe priced close to $4000, it sported bucket seats, vinyl roof, and distinctive exterior trim. First-year sales were so good that the Wildcat name replaced Invicta on all the big middle-series Buicks for '63 save a single wagon (fewer than 3500 sold), after which Invicta disappeared.

As noted, the premium Electra garnered steadily increasing sales throughout the Sixties. There were two series for 1960-61, both on a 126-inch wheelbase: a standard Electra and the larger, more luxurious Electra 225, named for its overall length in inches and known in some circles as the "Deuce-and-a-Quarter." This setup didn't last long, however, as the base series was dropped for '62 and all Electras became "225s." Buick then concentrated on fewer offerings. Electra's standard engine through 1966 was a 325-bhp 401 V-8. A bored-out 425 with 340/360 bhp became optionally available from 1964. Both then gave way to a standard 430 with 360 horses.

Buick styling wasn't exceptional in these years with the singular exception of the new-for-'63 Riviera, a svelte personal-luxury hardtop coupe that changed the division's

1960 LeSabre convertible coupe

1961 Electra four-door sedan

1961 Special four-door sedan

1962 Special Deluxe convertible coupe

1962 Electra 225 convertible coupe

1961 Skylark hardtop coupe

stodgy image almost overnight. Many felt that GM styling chief William L. Mitchell (who had succeeded Harley Earl on his retirement back in 1958) had shaped one of the all-time great automobiles.

Borrowing the name applied to Buick's earlier pillarless hardtops, the '63 Riviera was initially planned as a LaSalle, reviving Cadillac's lower-price companion make of 1927-40. Buick's Ned Nickles had designed an experimental "LaSalle II" roadster and hardtop sedan for the 1955 Motorama, both with trademark vertical-theme grille. But the real impetus toward "personal-luxury" was Ford's highly successful post-1957 four-seat Thunderbird. Ultimately, the final clay model approved in early 1961 as a new LaSalle was reassigned to Buick to give that division a much-needed shot in the sales arm. Besides, Cadillac didn't have the facilities to build this smaller car, Chevrolet was enjoying record popularity, and Oldsmobile and Pontiac were occupied with other matters.

Mitchell freely admitted to borrowing some of this new Riviera's design elements. Its razor-edge roof styling, for instance, was inspired by certain English custom coachwork of the Fifties. But the finished product was handsome and individual. As scheduled, production for model-year '63 was exactly 40,000.

Riding a 117-inch wheelbase, Riviera was about 14 inches shorter and 200-300 pounds lighter than other big Buicks. Initially, the Electra's 325-bhp 401 V-8 was standard and the new 340-bhp 425 optional. The latter became the base engine for '64, with a new 360-horsepower version available at extra cost. Standard two-speed Turbine Drive automatic was used for '63, three-speed Twin-Turbine Hydra-Matic afterwards. Handling was well up to the performance, which was formidable. The typical 325-bhp car could do the standing quarter-mile in 16 seconds at 85 mph; with 360 bhp, it improved to 15.5 seconds and 90-plus mph.

For 1964, Buick joined Olds and Pontiac in offering larger, restyled compacts, adopting the new intermediate-size GM A-body also used for that year's new Chevy Chevelle. Wheelbases stretched to 120 inches on wagons and 115 inches on other body styles. Engines were also new, with choices ranging from a 225-cid V-6 with 155 bhp to a cast-iron 300-cid V-8 with 210 or 250 bhp. Both Special and Skylark versions were again offered, but the plusher Skylark rapidly became the most popular smaller Buick: The Skylark-to-Special production ratio was about 9-to-10 for '64, after which Skylark pulled away, reaching a near 5-to-1 margin by 1969.

Flint's 1964 standards were longer overall but unchanged in wheelbase, and the new 300 V-8 became the base LeSabre powerplant. Like the old Century, Wildcat was the division's big hot rod, carrying the 401 Electra engine in the lighter, shorter LeSabre chassis. Reflecting its popularity, a four-door sedan joined the existing convertible and hardtops. All senior '64 Buicks retained their basic '63 look, but with corners and edges rounded off. Riviera was little changed in appearance, but production dropped by about 2500 units, partly due to stronger competition from a new-generation Thunderbird.

Buick's 1965 production was 137 percent above its 1960

1963 Riviera hardtop coupe

1963 Electra 225 convertible coupe

1963 Skylark sport coupe

1964 Skylark sport coupe

1964 Electra 225 hardtop coupe

total, putting the division fifth in the annual industry race. An expanded lineup in general and the unique Riviera in particular were responsible, but so was a very healthy overall market that bought Detroit cars in record numbers: over 9.3 million for the calendar year, the best since '55.

As elsewhere in Detroit, Buick proliferated trim and model variations for '65, allowing buyers to virtually custom-build their cars. That year's junior line comprised Skylarks and standard and Deluxe Specials with V-6 or V-8 power priced from about $2350-$3000, and V-8 Special "Sportwagons" in the $3000-$3200 range. Wildcat offered standard, Deluxe, and Custom trim in sedan, hardtop

sedan, and hardtop coupe styles, plus Deluxe and Custom convertibles; LeSabre and Electra 225 offered these body types in standard and Custom versions. At $4440 base, the Electra 225 Custom convertible remained the priciest Buick, with the elegant Riviera close behind at $4408. LeSabres still carried a standard 300 V-8, Wildcats and Electras the big 401. Rivieras gained added distinction in the form of hidden headlamps, the four beams being stacked vertically in upright pods (with rotating covers) mounted at the outer edges of the grill.

A memorable new performance option for '65 was the Gran Sport package for Riviera and Skylark, some $250

1964 Wildcat hardtop coupe

1965 LeSabre Custom hardtop coupe

1965 Skylark Sports Wagon

1966 Riviera GS hardtop coupe

1967 Skylark four-door sedan

worth of roadability improvements. With oversize tires, heavy-duty suspension, and Wildcat 401 V-8, the Skylark Gran Sport was every inch a grand touring car, though it was really Buick's "muscle car" reply to the Pontiac GTO. The GS Riviera was even grander in its way, capable of 125 mph flat out.

Buick's main attraction for 1966 was a second-generation Riviera, a cousin to that year's new E-body front-drive Olds Toronado. The Riv retained rear drive and looked much more massive than the crisp 1963-65 original, yet wheelbase was only two inches longer. Curvaceous new contours, wide hidden-headlamp grille, and a sleek semi-fastback profile with vestiges of the previous razor-edge roof made it impressive to the eye. Yet it sold for only about $4400, which seems unbelievably low today.

Other '66 Buicks were mainly carryovers, but a stroked 340-cid version of the 300 V-8 was issued as standard power for LeSabres and Skylark Sportwagons. Modestly redone grilles, side trim, and taillights were again the principal alterations for the '67 juniors, but that year's senior Buicks were treated to GM's new B- and C-bodies, with sleek semi-fastback roof styling for hardtop coupes and more voluptuous contours across the board. Identifying the '67 Riviera was a horizontal-crossbar grille and redesigned parking lights.

Specials and Skylarks continued with the 225 V-6 and 300/340 V-8s for '67, but a new 430 V-8—Buick's biggest engine yet—arrived as standard for Wildcat, Electra, and Riviera. Though no more potent than the previous 425, it was smoother and quieter. The Skylark Gran Sport was renamed GS400, and a virtually identical car with the 340 engine appeared as the GS340. Overall, Buick sales were excellent: more than 560,000 units for the model year.

Skylark sold in record numbers for 1968, partly because Specials were trimmed to just three Deluxe models. Like other GM intermediates that year, Buick's junior line adopted a new "split-wheelbase" A-body platform, making for 112-inch Special/Skylark two-doors, 116-inch Special four-doors and Deluxe wagons, and 121-inch Sportwagons (versus 120 inches for 1964-67 wagons). The hot GS400 returned as a hardtop and convertible. Replacing the GS340 was a GS350 hardtop with a newly bored 350-cid V-8 delivering 280 bhp. A 230-bhp rendition was a new Special/Skylark option and standard for Sportwagon, Skylark Custom, and LeSabres; all these offered the tuned unit at extra cost. The 225 V-6 gave way to a Chevy-built 250 inline six with lower compression, reflecting 1968's new federal emissions rules. The big 430, still pumping out a nominal 360 bhp, remained standard for Wildcat, Electra, and Riviera.

Like the '67s, Buick's 1968 seniors had bodyside sculpturing (traced with moldings on some models) recalling the old Fifties "sweepspear," plus divided grilles, big bumpers and, new that season, hidden wipers. The rebodied junior models had similar down-sloped bodyside contour lines, plus new grilles, the hidden wipers, pointy rear fenders, and big back bumpers containing the taillamps. Riviera got a dubious, heavy-handed divided grille that made it a bit more contrived than in 1966-67. Many Buicks maintained tradition with stylized front-fender "ventiports," a trade-

1968 GS 350 hardtop coupe

1968 LeSabre Custom convertible coupe

1969 Electra 225 hardtop coupe

1969 GS 400 convertible coupe

1969 Riviera hardtop coupe

1969 Sport Wagon

mark dating from the Forties. Exceptions were Wildcats, GS400s, and uplevel Skylark Customs, where rectangular trim was used to suggest air vents of various types.

No engine changes occurred for record-breaking 1969, when Buick built more than 665,000 cars, though it still finished fifth in the industry. Seniors again received new bodies, this time with ventless side glass and a squarer, more "formal" look. The year-old junior line displayed the expected minor trim shuffles; Gran Sports and Sport-

wagons remained ostensibly separate series, as in 1968. LeSabre was still on its 123-inch wheelbase, but so was Wildcat again, for the first time in four years.

Buicks of the Sixties were remarkably consistent in design and engineering. That the division needed no sensational breakthroughs (other than perhaps the Riviera) to more than double its volume in this decade is testament to the soundness of its basic planning and the value of its products.

BUICK AT A GLANCE, 1960-1969										
	1960	**1961**	**1962**	**1963**	**1964**	**1965**	**1966**	**1967**	**1968**	**1969**
Price Range, $	2756-4300	2330-4350	2304-4448	2309-4365	2343-4385	2343-4440	2348-4424	2411-4469	2513-4615	2562-4701
Weight Range, lbs.	4139-4653	2579-4441	2638-4505	2661-4397	2991-4362	2977-4344	3009-4323	3071-4336	3185-4314	3182-4328
Wheelbases, in.	123-126.3	112-126	112-126	112-126	115-126	115-126	115-126	115-126	112-126	112-126.2
6 Cyl. Engines, hp			135	135	155	155	160	160	155	155
8 Cyl. Engines, hp	235-325	155-325	155-325	155-325	210-360	210-360	210-340	210-360	230-360	230-360

CADILLAC

Having become America's undisputed luxury leader well before the Sixties, Cadillac maintained its sales supremacy by continuing to emphasize mechanical refinement and the latest comfort and convenience features. Yet perhaps more of its great success in these years was owed to styling that became progressively more graceful and restrained, though still recognizably Cadillac. Nowhere was the turn from Fifties flamboyance to conservative good taste more evident than in the gradual shrinking of Cadillac's famous tailfins; having reached mountainous proportions for 1959, they would be all but gone six years later.

The Sixties brought few engineering advances of the sort that had earned Cadillac such great renown during the previous 20 years. Its most technically interesting car of this decade was the front-drive Eldorado, introduced for 1967. The smallest Cadillac since the last 1940 LaSalle, it combined mechanical innovation with traditional Cadillac lines that still look good today.

But it was consistently good styling across the broadest model line in the luxury field that helped Cadillac to new sales records most every year during the Sixties. The company's gradual transition from glittery excess to stately elegance seemed to anticipate the luxury buyer's tastes.

The cleanup began right away with a facelifted 1960 line bearing simpler grilles and lower-profile fins. Offerings stayed the same, as did prices, ranging from $4892 for the Series 62 hardtop coupe to $9748 for the big Series 75 limousine. Mechanical specifications also stood pat. Standard horsepower remained 325, with 345 reserved for the Eldorado Biarritz convertible and Seville hardtop coupe, both courtesy of the 390-cubic-inch V-8 introduced for 1959.

Series 62 remained the volume leader, but the mid-range DeVille, another '59 development, was coming on strong. As before, both series had no pillared sedans but did offer two hardtop four-doors: a flat-top "Vista roof" job with

radically wrapped backlight, and a more conventional "six-window" style with rear-door ventpanes. Returning for its final year was the Eldorado Brougham hardtop sedan, unchanged from '59 as an evolution of the intriguing but unsuccessful 1957-58 model. Still priced at a towering $13,075 but now boasting bodywork by Pininfarina of Italy, it sold only 101 copies in 1960—less than even the original Brougham's 704. Worse, they were built nowhere near as well. Overall, Cadillac remained 10th in model-year production for 1960 (a position held since '58) and would remain there through 1964, though that was still impressive for a luxury make.

Carrying another new GM C-body, the '61s were the cleanest Cadillacs in years. They were also the first influenced by William L. Mitchell, who had been installed as GM design chief in 1958. Mitchell favored a more chiseled look than his predecessor, Harley Earl, and wasn't as enamored of chrome. Grilles became a prominent grid, while fins were trimmed again. The Eldorado Seville disappeared with the Brougham, while the Biarritz was downgraded to the standard 325-bhp V-8.

With GM settling into a styling groove, Cadillac's '62s were basically toned-down '61s. Highlights included still-lower fins, front-fender cornering lights as a new option, a somewhat tamer grille, and backup/turn/stop lights combined behind a single white lens. Four-window sedans received more orthodox rooflines but still included a pair of short-deck variants, which were now named Series 62 Town Sedan and DeVille Park Avenue. A new braking system with dual master cylinder and separate front and rear hydraulic lines appeared, a portent of the future. Model-year output rose to nearly 161,000, up some 23,000 over '61.

Cadillac's long-running V-8 got its first major revision in 14 years for 1963. Bore and stroke were unchanged, as were valves, rocker arms, cylinder heads, compression (still

1960 Eldorado Biarritz convertible coupe

10.5:1), and connecting rods. But nearly everything else was different: lighter, stronger crankshaft; a stiffer block weighing 50 pounds less than the previous one; ancillaries relocated to improve service access. While all this did little for performance, the revised 390 was much smoother and quieter. Then again, performance was already good. The typical '63 could reach 115-120 mph, do 0-60 mph in 10 seconds, and return about 14 miles per gallon. Most impressive was the near-silence at high speed. In this, many testers held Cadillac superior to Rolls-Royce. Styling departed from recent practice. Fins were lower than ever, the grille was bulkier, new outer body panels and side moldings created a more slab-sided effect, and the rear was more massive, with elongated vertical tail/backup-light housings.

Prices rose only slightly for '63, so Cadillac remained an excellent value for the money. Standard equipment ran to Hydra-Matic, power steering, self-adjusting power brakes, heater, backup lights, and left remote-control door mirror. A six-way power seat became standard on Eldorado, and power windows were included on all except Series 62 sedans and coupes. Even power vent windows were offered, as were vinyl roof coverings, a new option. Remarkably, a Series 62 still cost as little as $5026; the Eldo Biarritz was only $6608. Production topped 163,000.

Design revisions for '64 were minor. Even lower tailfins created a straight-through beltline, accentuating length; grilles got a body-color horizontal bar; and taillamp housings were reshaped. A new automatic heating/air-conditioning system maintained a set temperature regardless of outside conditions—a Cadillac feature ever since. More significant was a 390 bored and stroked to 429 cid, good for 340 bhp. Unit volume improved to near 166,000.

Cadillac had a resounding 1965, producing close to 200,000 cars. But it was a banner year for all Detroit, so that was only good for 11th place. The "budget" Series 62, a fixture since 1940, was renamed Calais. Eldorado and the Sixty Special were officially Fleetwoods, like Series 75, bearing the requisite nameplates, wreath-and-crest medallions, broad rocker panel and rear-quarter brightwork, and rectangular-pattern rear appliqués. A new Fleetwood Brougham sedan, actually a Sixty Special trim option, offered a vinyl roof with rear-quarter "Brougham" script.

Another body change gave the '65s a longer, lower silhouette, with fins planed absolutely flat, though a hint of them remained. Also new were a straight back bumper and vertical lamp clusters. Up front, headlight pairs switched from horizontal to vertical, thus permitting an even wider grille. Curved side windows appeared, and pillared sedans returned in the Calais and DeVille series. Sixty Specials likewise gained roof pillars, while six-window hardtop sedans were dropped. The Special also reverted to its exclusive 133-inch wheelbase after riding the standard 129.5-inch chassis for 1959-64.

Though Cadillac's V-8 was unchanged, the slightly lighter '65s offered the luxury market's best power-to-weight ratio. "Dual driving range" Turbo Hydra-Matic and full-perimeter frames (replacing the X-type used since '57) were adopted except for 75s, and all models came with a new "sonically balanced" exhaust system. Amazingly, prices weren't far above what they'd been in '61.

1960 Coupe de Ville hardtop coupe

1961 Eldorado Biarritz convertible coupe

1962 Eldorado Biarritz convertible coupe

1963 Eldorado Biarritz convertible coupe

1963 Sedan de Ville four-window hardtop sedan

1964 Eldorado Biarritz convertible coupe

1964 Fleetwood limousine

1968 Eldorado hardtop coupe

1965 de Ville convertible coupe

1966 de Ville convertible coupe

Cadillac enjoyed its first 200,000-car year for calendar '66, breaking the barrier by precisely 5001 units. A mild facelift brought a new front bumper and grille, plus more integrated taillight housings. The 75 switched to the new perimeter frame and was fully restyled for the first time since 1959. Variable-ratio power steering was a new option, as were carbon-cloth seat heating pads. The Fleetwood Brougham became a separate model, still more luxuriously trimmed than the plain-roof Sixty Special and priced about $320 higher.

The most significant Cadillac of the decade arrived for 1967: an all-new Eldorado with front-wheel drive. Based on the previous year's new Oldsmobile Toronado, it was a daring concept for the luxury field, with six years of careful planning and research behind it. Front drive gave it outstanding roadability; Bill Mitchell gave it magnificent styling.

It had originated in 1959 with the XP-727 program, which underwent several design alterations through early 1962. Management then settled on front-wheel drive, and further prototypes evolved with that in mind. For awhile, Cadillac considered calling it LaSalle, but ultimately chose Eldorado as a more current name with greater public recognition. Clay model XP-825, with razor-edge lines and a formal roofline, led directly to the production '67 coupe.

Unlike Toronado, this new Eldorado was announced in very low-key fashion. That was typical of Cadillac, as was using a one-year delay to improve on a sister division's work. The Eldo thus rode better than the Toronado, yet handled at least as well despite the same basic suspension: torsion bars, A-arms, and telescopic shocks in front; a beam axle on semi-elliptic leaf springs with four shock absorbers (two horizontal, two vertical) at the rear. Self-leveling control and radially vented front disc brakes were also featured.

On its own relatively compact 120-inch wheelbase, the front-drive Eldorado was announced at $6277 and targeted for 10 percent of Cadillac's total 1967 model-year production—about 20,000 units. The final figure was 17,930. For 1968-70, sales ran 23,000-28,000. A technological *tour de force*, it quickly established itself as the ultimate Cadillac. And unlike the old Fifties Brougham, it made money from day one.

Cadillac's 1967 "standards" were treated to an extensive restyle, with forward-angled headlamps and a prominent hump over the rear wheels. Line-wide features included printed mylar instrument-panel circuits, automatic level control (standard on Fleetwoods), cruise control, and tilt steering wheel. Bolstered by the new Eldorado, also part of the Fleetwood series, Cadillac built precisely 200,000 cars for the model year.

The 1968 spotlight was on motive power: an all-new 472-cid V-8 with 375 bhp. Designed to meet the new government emission standards that took effect that year, it was extensively tested in the laboratory, being run the equivalent of 500,000 miles. Though not as fuel-efficient as its predecessor, the 472 could boast of being the largest production engine offered in the industry.

Designwise, the '68 Eldorado gained the federally required side marker lights, plus larger taillights, combined turn signal/parking lamps nested in the front-fender caps, and a hood extended at the rear to conceal the windshield wipers. Standards also got the hidden wipers and side markers, along with a revised grille.

Cadillac built a record 266,798 cars for calendar 1969, enough to grab ninth place in the industry rankings. For the model year, though, it was still 11th at a little over 223,000, down some 7,000 units from '68.

Eldorado was much the same as before, except that headlights were no longer hidden behind flip-up grille panels. Standards were restyled fore and aft, the major change being a return to horizontal headlamps. Parking lights wrapped around the front fenders and flanked a taller grille, still prominently vee'd. A somewhat unpopular change was the elimination of front vent windows. Per

Washington edict, no-cost equipment now included front headrests, energy-absorbing steering column, pushbutton seatbelt buckles, ignition-key warning buzzer, and anti-theft steering column/transmission lock. Prices ran from just above $5400 for a Calais to well over $10,000 for the 75 limousine.

Though hardly the innovator it had been in years past (the Eldorado notwithstanding), Cadillac made all the right moves during the Sixties. Offering its renowned combination of luxury, performance, and style, the company managed to defend its title as "Standard of the World"—or at least of America. While its return to more conservative styling actually lagged behind the rest of the industry, it seems only proper that the company responsible for giving birth to the tailfin should also be the last to abandon it.

1967 Eldorado hardtop coupe

1967 de Ville convertible coupe

1968 de Ville convertible coupe

1969 Eldorado hardtop coupe

CADILLAC AT A GLANCE, 1960-1969										
	1960	1961	1962	1963	1964	1965	1966	1967	1968	1969
Price Range, $	4892-13,075	4892-9748	5025-9937	5026-9939	5048-9960	5059-9960	4986-10,521	5040-10,571	5315-10,768	5484-10,979
Weight Range, lbs.	4670-5560	4560-5420	4530-5390	4505-5300	4475-5300	4435-5260	4390-5435	4447-5436	4570-5385	4550-5555
Wheelbases, in.	130-149.8	129.5-149.8	129.5-149.8	129.5-149.8	129.5-149.8	129.5-149.8	129.5-149.8	129.5-149.8	129.5-149.8	129.5-149.8
8 Cyl. Engines, hp	325-345	325	325	325	340	340	340	340	375	375

CHECKER

Checker was long known for taxicabs and airport limousines when it began marketing "civilian" versions in 1960. Initially called Superba, they were offered as four-door sedans and wagons in standard and Special trim. The latter were more deluxe inside but not much. All were the same tank-like affairs familiar to anyone who'd ever hailed a Checker cab. Wheelbase was 120 inches, fairly compact for the day. Curb weights ranged from around 3400 pounds for sedans to near 3800 pounds for wagons.

Morris Markin, Checker's founder and president, was adamant: There'd be no change to this dumpy but practical design so long as there were buyers for reliable, durable "taxi-tough" cars. Not that there'd been many changes before. In fact, the Superba dated from Checker's A8 taxicab of 1956.

Checker power through 1964 came from Continental Motor Company, basically the same 226-cubic-inch L-head six that Kaiser had used. Interestingly, though, Checker offered it in both side-valve and overhead-valve form. The former produced a mere 80 horsepower on 7.3:1 compression; the latter had 8.0:1 compression and a more respectable 122 bhp. Both cost exactly the same.

True to their taxi heritage, Superbas came with a pair of rear jump seats and could carry up to eight. The wagon's rear seat folded up or down by means of an electronic servo controlled from the dashboard. This gimmick and differ-

ent bodywork made the wagon about $350 more than the sedan.

For 1961, the Superba Special was renamed Marathon, the sedan's 15-inch wheels were replaced by 14-inchers for slightly lower ride height, and the ohv six became standard for wagons. Prices stood pat: $2542 for the Superba sedan to $3004 for the Marathon wagon. Air conditioning cost $411 extra, power steering $64. Like Checker cabs, the Superba/Marathon had a full bank of gauges, a spartan but well-padded interior, wide doors, and a spacious rear compartment.

This quartet continued for 1962, the only change being a return to 15-inch wheels for sedans. However, there was now a special Town Custom limousine on a 129-inch wheelbase, optimistically priced at $7500. Vinyl roof and even a glassed-in driver's compartment were standard, and there was a full range of power options. But demand was low—understandable, as even the most expensive non-limousine Cadillac cost less. The ohv engine was booted to 141 bhp for all '63 models.

Prices were about $100 higher for '64, and the Superba name was dropped. Checker switched to Chevrolet engines for 1965: 230-cid, 140-bhp six; 195-bhp 283 V-8; 250-bhp 327 V-8. The Town Custom limo was still around, but only through special order. The 283 engine cost $110 extra, automatic transmission $248, and overdrive $108.

For 1966, Checker added a Marathon Deluxe sedan and a lower-priced limousine ($4541), thus reestablishing its four-model lineup. Both were dropped the following year, but the Deluxe sedan returned for '68; the limousine for '69.

With their Chevy V-8s, post-1964 Checkers were naturally much faster than the earlier six-cylinder jobs, and they became even more potent later on. The 283 option was dropped for '67 and a 307-cid replacement with 200 bhp arrived the following year. For 1969, the 327 gave way to Chevy's new 350-cid enlargement with 300 bhp. Emissions tuning cut that to 250 bhp for 1970. Prices for the optional engines were usually low: for 1968, $108 for the 307 and $195 for the 327.

Checker sales were always moderate in the Sixties, though adequate to sustain the firm's desired annual volume of 6000-7000 units. Checker's best performance of the decade came in 1962 with 8173 units, though most of these were taxis.

Markin never wavered from his mission of building taxi-tough cars. Nor did son David, who took over the reins upon the founder's death in 1970. But the lack of change would prove fatal a dozen years later, when Checker closed its doors in the face of ever-increasing fleet-sales competition from Detroit, as well as its own relatively high overhead, low production capacity, and minuscule resources for developing new products. Passenger-car output was dramatically lower after 1969: fewer than 400 for 1970, 600-1000 units a year through 1974, less than 500 thereafter.

Left stillborn was a new-design Checker devised under Edward N. Cole, who went to Kalamazoo after retiring as GM president in 1974. Slated for a 1983 release, it was a boxy four-door hatchback sedan with front-drive mechanicals to be borrowed from the GM X-car compacts that

1966 Marathon four-door sedan

1966 Marathon taxi

Cole knew were in the works. A sturdy box-section chassis of undisclosed design was planned for three wheelbases and six-, eight-, and nine-passenger models. A variety of low-cost, easily replaced plastic body panels was considered, as was an interesting rear suspension with solid rubber springs. The project got as far as a single full-scale mockup, then lost momentum with Cole's untimely death in a plane crash. By that time, even Checker's taxi business had become marginal, and the firm ended all production in mid-1982.

1960 Superba four-door sedan

1960 Superba four-door sedan

1960 Superba four-door sedan

CHECKER AT A GLANCE, 1960-1969										
	1960	**1961**	**1962**	**1963**	**1964**	**1965**	**1966**	**1967**	**1968**	**1969**
Price Range, $	2542-3004	2542-3004	2642-7500	2642-7500	2814-8500	2793-8000	2874-4541	2874-3075	3221-3913	3290-4969
Weight Range, lbs.	3410-3780	3320-3615	3320-3615	3485-5000	3485-5000	3360-4800	3400-3800	3400-3500	3390-3590	3390-3802
Wheelbases, in.	120	120	120-129	120-129	120-129	120-129	120	120	120	120-129
6 Cyl. Engines, hp	80-122	80-122	80-122	80-141	80-141	140	140	140	140	155
8 Cyl. Engines, hp						195-250	195-250	250	200-275	235-300

CHEVROLET

During the Fifties and Sixties, Ford frequently got the jump on Chevrolet when it came to innovative new products, but Chevy remained the low-price production leader, winning every model-year race save 1961 and 1966. Like its arch rival, the division expanded into compacts (Corvair and Chevy II), intermediates (Chevelle), muscle cars (Malibu SS, Impala SS), full-size luxury-liners (Caprice), and "ponycars" (Camaro). Each was carefully conceived to fill a basic need (and market slot), and nearly all succeeded. (Corvair and the Corvette sports car are different enough to be treated separately in this book.)

Such increasing specialization might imply increasing production, but even though Chevy did set some records, its 1969 volume was "only" some 500,000 cars ahead of 1960's despite the interim addition of four new model lines. The proliferation came in response to a market that subdivided, generating more "niche" competition than in the Fifties. In many cases, Chevy competed less against Ford than against itself or other GM divisions.

Standard Chevrolets moved quickly from overstyled outrageousness to smooth, crisp elegance. The 1960 models were basically a carry-over from the previous year, but a facelift left them cleaner and more subdued than the "batwing" '59s. Taut new finless styling arrived for '61, then a heavier, more sculptured look for '62. With no change in wheelbase, the big Chevy became bulkier as the decade progressed, but was still deftly styled. Another complete redesign brought more flowing lines for '65, followed by an even curvier all-new '67 body with semi-fastback hardtop coupe rooflines and more pronounced "Coke bottle" fenders. A still-huskier appearance was achieved for 1969 via elliptical wheel openings and subtle bulges. This era's prettiest big Chevy might well be the '62, with its straight, cor-

1960 Impala Sport Sedan

rect lines and, for Impala hardtop coupes, a roofline simulating a raised convertible top.

Nineteen sixty-two also saw Chevy enlarge its 283 small-block V-8 to 327 cid, offering an initial 250 to 300 bhp in the full-size cars. However, 283s would continue to power a variety of Chevys through 1967, when a stroked 350 was introduced that was more amenable to the newly-legislated emissions standards.

Biscayne remained Chevy's full-size price leader in the Sixties, though buyer interest quickly tapered off. The mid-priced Bel Air also waned. The top-line Impala, however, rapidly became Detroit's single most popular model line. Its best sales year in this decade was 1964, with some 889,600 built.

By far the most collectible Impala is the performance-bred Super Sport, an option package for mid-1961 and 1968-69, an Impala sub-series in other years. Body styles were always limited to convertible and hardtop coupe. The

1960 Impala Sport Coupe

18

1961 Impala Sport Coupe

1961 Impala Sport Sedan

concept was simple: the big, smooth Chevy with sporty touches inside and out and available performance and handling options. Sixes were offered but not usually ordered (only 3600 of the '65s, for instance). Typical features ran to SS emblems, vinyl front bucket seats, central gearshift console, and optional tachometer. A variety of V-8s was offered, including big-blocks, beginning with the famous 409 of 1961. This was an enlarged version of the 348 (introduced for '58) delivering 360 bhp initially and up to 425 bhp by '63. With options like stiffer springs and shocks, sintered-metallic brake linings, four-speed gearbox, and quick-ratio power steering, these were the best-performing big Chevys in history. Unfortunately, they wouldn't last. Government regulations and the advent of mid-size "muscle cars" combined to render large sporty cars obsolete. Yet the Impala SS remained exciting right to the end, offering the 427-cid "Mark IV" engine from 1967 with 335-385 bhp.

Meanwhile, Chevrolet uncovered a far more lucrative market by dolling up the Impala with the best grades of upholstery and trim and calling it Caprice. A mid-1965 arrival, it garnered some 181,000 sales for model year '66, when it became a separate series, and the original hardtop sedan was joined by wagons and a hardtop coupe. Production through the rest of the decade ranged from 115,500 to nearly 167,000. Obviously, Cadillac luxury at Chevy prices still had as much appeal in the Sixties as it had in the late Fifties with the first Impala.

A rung below the standards was the intermediate Chevelle, introduced for 1964 as a reply to Ford's Fairlane. Conventional in design—front engine, rear drive, front coil springs, rear leaf springs—it offered almost as much interior room as an Impala but within more sensible exterior dimensions. In effect, Chevelle was a revival of the ideally proportioned "classic" Chevy of 1955-57. Sales went nowhere but up, from an initial 328,400 units to

1961 Impala convertible coupe

1962 Chevy II Nova 400 convertible coupe

1962 Impala Sport Coupe

1963 Impala Sport Coupe

1960. Initial engine choices were a 90-bhp 153-cid four and a 120-bhp 194-cid six. (Falcon had only sixes through mid-1963, then added a small-block V-8 option.) It was a good move, but through 1966, Chevy IIs outnumbered Falcons only once: model year '63. Sales dropped nearly 50 percent for '64, due partly to intramural competition from Chevelle. A spate of Super Sport models didn't help. Nor did heavy facelifts for '65 and '66.

For 1968, Chevy II grew to near intermediate size, switching to GM's all-new 111-inch-wheelbase X-body platform, which actually had much in common with that year's new mid-size cars. Convertibles, wagons, and hardtop coupes were deleted, leaving only semi-fastback pillared coupes and four-door sedans. The former were available in SS trim, now a package option. Backed by a strong ad campaign and competitive prices, Chevy's compact made a comeback, sales soaring to 201,000 units for '68 and to over a quarter-million by 1970, by which time the name was Nova (originally, the premium Chevy II series).

Adding spice to the line for 1967 was Camaro, which would eventually succeed the ailing Corvair as Chevy's sporty compact. Despite the beautiful styling and impressive performance of the all-new '65 models, Corvair was still no threat to Ford's incredibly successful Mustang in the burgeoning "ponycar" market. Worse, it was costly to build, being entirely different in concept and technology from other Chevrolets. Six months after the '65s debuted, division managers decreed that Corvair should be allowed to fade away. Camaro would be its replacement—a conventional front-engine sporty car, a direct Mustang-fighter.

Created under the watchful eye of GM design chief Bill Mitchell, Camaro styling was exactly right: long-hood/short-deck proportions; a low, chiseled profile; flowing

1963 Chevy II Nova SS Sport Coupe

1963 Biscayne wagon

nearly 440,000 by 1969. The addition of numerous performance options, including Malibu SS convertible and hardtop, only enhanced Chevelle's appeal.

Third down the size scale was the Chevy II, an orthodox compact rushed out for 1962 to answer Ford's Falcon, which had been handily outselling the radical Corvair since

1964 Impala SS Sport Coupe

1964 Chevelle Malibu SS convertible coupe

1964 Chevy II Nova four-door sedan

1965 Chevy II Nova SS hardtop coupe

1965 Impala wagon

body lines. Like Mustang, Camaro aimed at those who wanted a sporty four-seater that could be equipped as an economy runabout, vivid straightline performer, or something in between, so there was a Mustang-like plethora of options: some 81 factory items and 41 dealer-installed accessories.

Initial Camaro prices were $2466 for the basic hardtop coupe and $2704 for the convertible with standard 140-bhp six. A 155-bhp, 250-cid six cost $26 extra; the 210-bhp 327 V-8 listed for $106. Next up was a 350-cid V-8 with 295 bhp, exclusive to Camaro for '67 (though it soon became the most popular Corvette engine). But to get it, you had to

1965 Chevelle Malibu SS hardtop coupe

1965 Caprice hardtop sedan

1966 Impala SS hardtop coupe

1966 Chevelle SS hardtop coupe

1966 Impala convertible coupe

1967 Camaro Z-28 hardtop coupe

1967 Chevy II Nova SS hardtop coupe

order the $211 Super Sports package comprising stiffer springs and shocks, D70-14 Firestone Wide Oval tires, modified hood with extra sound insulation, SS emblems, and "bumblebee" nose stripes. A 396 big-block became available later in the year at nearly $400.

Also tempting Camaro buyers: custom carpeting, front bucket seats, fold-down back seat, luxury interior, full gauges, and console shifters. A $105 Rally Sport package

1967 Impala hardtop coupe

added a hidden-headlight grille, special emblems, and other touches. Additional extras included tinted glass, radios, heater, air conditioning, clock, cruise control, and a vinyl roof cover for hardtops. Mechanical options ran to sintered-metallic brake linings, vented front-disc brakes, vacuum brake booster, power steering, quick-ratio manual steering, stiff suspension, Positraction limited-slip differential, and a dozen different axle ratios. With all this, a Camaro could easily be boosted to $5000.

Though two years behind Mustang, Camaro was a big hit. Production topped 220,000 the first year, followed by 235,115 for '68 and another 243,095 for '69. There were no major changes through early 1970. The '68s sported a modified grille, restyled taillamps, ventless side glass, and flow-through "Astro Ventilation." (The last two appeared throughout most of the Chevy line save Corvair and Chevy II.) The '69s had a recontoured lower body with front and rear creaselines above the wheel openings, plus a vee'd grille and new rear styling.

Available for the street but aimed squarely at the track was Regular Production Option Z28, a tailor-made road-racing package announced during 1967. With it, Camaro won 18 of 25 Trans-Am races, then the class championship in 1968 and '69. Veteran competition engineer Vincent W.

1968 Chevelle SS 396 hardtop coupe

1968 Camaro SS hardtop coupe

1967 Chevelle SS hardtop coupe

1968 Impala SS 427 convertible coupe

1969 Impala SS 427 convertible coupe

1969 Chevelle Malibu hardtop coupe

Piggins had convinced management to build a Camaro expressly for that new Sports Car Club of America series. To meet its prevailing displacement limit, he combined a 327 block with a 283 crankshaft to produce a high-winding 302.4-cid small-block with a nominal 290 bhp—it was more like 350—and 290 pounds/feet torque. Completing the package were heavy-duty suspension, front-disc brakes, metallic rear brake linings, 11-inch clutch, close-ratio four-speed, quick steering, wide Corvette wheels, and hood air ducts feeding big carburetors.

At an initial $3300 or so, the Z28 was a whale of a high-performance buy. It wasn't for everyone, of course, but production quickly climbed, from 602 of the '67s to 7199 for '68 and 20,302 of the '69s. All are now coveted collectibles, not only as the first of a great breed but also because the Z would become less special in future years.

CHEVROLET AT A GLANCE, 1960-1969										
	1960	1961	1962	1963	1964	1965	1966	1967	1968	1969
Price Range, $	2175-2996	2175-3099	2003-3171	2003-3170	2011-3196	2011-3212	2028-3347	2090-3413	2222-3570	2237-3678
Weight Range, lbs.	3455-4000	3390-3935	2410-3925	2430-3870	2455-3895	2505-4005	2520-4020	2555-3990	2760-4005	2785-4300
Wheelbases, in.	119	119	110-119	110-119	110-119	110-119	110-119	108-119	108-119	108-119
4 Cyl. Engines, hp			90	90	90	90	90	90	90	90
6 Cyl. Engines, hp	135	135	120-135	120-140	120-155	120-150	120-155	120-155	140-155	140-155
8 Cyl. Engines, hp	170-335	170-360	170-409	195-425	195-425	195-425	195-425	195-385	200-425	200-425

Corvair was the most controversial Chevrolet since the abortive 1923 "Copper-Cooled" model. Of course, neither was *supposed* to stir up trouble; each was merely a response to a particular market situation of its day. The problem with Corvair was a radical design that made it too costly and "foreign" for its target audience, though it found temporary salvation by opening up an entirely different market, almost by accident. And that's the irony, for Corvair's success as a sporty compact spawned the car that would later help do it in: the Ford Mustang. A young lawyer-on-the-make named Ralph Nader did the rest.

Chevrolet's interest in a smaller, companion car was evident as early as the mid-Forties, when it developed the Cadet, a prototype 2200-pound four-door sedan of conventional design. Powered by a short-stroke 133-cubic-inch six, this 108-inch-wheelbase compact was intended to sell at a rock-bottom price in anticipation of a postwar recession. But the market boomed instead, rendering Cadet unnecessary. Besides, it would have cost about as much to build as a regular Chevy, and would thus have proved unprofitable at the $1000 target retail price. The project was duly canceled in mid-1947.

Things were far different by the late Fifties. Led by Volkswagen and Renault, sales of economy imports were becoming too large to ignore, particularly once a national recession hit in mid-1957. American Motors responded with its compact 1958 American, a warmed-over Nash Rambler. Studebaker chimed in with its similar '59 Lark, which was so successful that it temporarily halted that firm's slide to oblivion. Both cars would soon have rivals. Ford was readying its Falcon and Chrysler its Valiant for 1960. General Motors, which in 1958-59 turned to so-called "captive imports" (Vauxhall and Opel), would rely on the Corvair.

Initiated in 1956, the Corvair was largely the product of Chevy chief engineer (and future GM president) Edward N. Cole, who became division general manager in July of that year. It was predictably a technician's car, by far the most *avant garde* of the new Big Three compacts. Perhaps inspired by Cole's interest in airplanes—but more likely by the popular VW Beetle—it was planned around a 140-cid air-cooled flat-six developing 80 or 95 horsepower in initial form and—just as uncommon—mounted at the rear ("where an engine belongs," ads would claim). Quite complicated for a low-priced car, it had six separate cylinder barrels and a divided crankcase. Yet despite a lightweight aluminum block, the engine ended up at 366 pounds, some 78 pounds above projections, a miscalculation that would have a profoundly negative effect on handling.

All-independent suspension and unit construction were equally unusual for a U.S. car. Corvair's trim 108-inch-wheelbase Y-body platform was all-new, but its all-coil suspension was perhaps too basic: conventional wishbones in front, Beetle-style semi-trailing swing axles in back. Antisway bars were omitted to keep retail price as low as possible, but this saved only $4 a car, and GM was well aware that the bars were needed to achieve acceptable handling with rear swing axles and the tail-heavy weight distribution. This decision, as well as management's desire to standardize assembly, precluded more sophisticated chassis components until 1962, when a regular production option

with stiffer springs, shorter rear-axle limit straps, and a front sway bar was made available. A major suspension improvement occurred for 1964: a rear transverse camber-compensating spring.

Nevertheless, the 1960-63 suspension did not create a "dangerous, ill-handling car" as later lawsuits claimed. Early Corvairs did oversteer, but the tendency was not excessive—provided recommended tire pressures were observed (15 psi front, 26 rear). The problem was that most owners didn't pay attention to that and some got into trouble. When Ralph Nader found out and wrote *Unsafe At Any Speed*, Corvair handling became a *cause celebre* that wasn't settled until a 1972 Congressional inquiry cleared the 1960-63 models. But by then, of course, it was too late. Corvair had been laid to rest three years before.

Corvair's 10-year model run neatly divides into two design generations: 1960-64 and 1965-69. Initial offerings comprised quite spartan four-door sedans in 500 and more deluxe 700 trim selling at $2000-$2100. Three-speed floorshift manual transaxle was standard; Chevy's two-speed Powerglide was optional. Two-door 500 and 700 coupes arrived at mid-season, but the real attention-getter was the new 900 Monza coupe, which boasted an even spiffier interior with bucket seats.

For 1961, Chevy offered an optional four-speed gearbox and the Monza caught fire, uncovering a huge, latent demand for sporty, fun-to-drive compacts. This was fortunate, because Ford's much simpler and cheaper Falcon was handily outselling other Corvairs in the economy market. With the Monza, Corvair aimed increasingly at enthusiast drivers.

But it was too late to change some plans, so a brace of Lakewood station wagons arrived as scheduled for '61, as did a Monza sedan. Lakewoods offered a surprising amount of cargo space—58 cubic feet behind the front seat, an additional 10 under the front "hood"—more than other compact wagons and even some larger ones. It didn't sell well, though, first-year production barely topping 25,000 units. Chevy also issued the interesting Corvair-based Greenbrier window van, Corvan panel, and Rampside pickup, all with a "forward control" design doubtless inspired by VW's Type 2 Microbus and forerunners of today's popular minivans. Finally, the flat-six was bored out to 145 cid. Standard power remained at 80, but a $27 "Turbo Air" option offered 98.

For 1962, the 500 series was trimmed to a single coupe, while the Monza line expanded to include the wagon (no longer called Lakewood) and a new convertible. The Monza wagon was plush, but only about 6000 were built before the body style was dropped entirely to make room on the assembly line for the Chevy II, a resolutely orthodox Falcon-style compact that Chevy rushed out to do what Corvair had failed to as an economy car.

Mid-1962 brought what has become the most highly prized first-generation Corvair: the turbocharged Monza Spyder. Initially, this was a $317 option package for Monza two-doors comprising a 150-bhp engine, shorter final drive for sprightlier acceleration, heavy-duty suspension, and a multi-gauge instrument panel with tachometer. The four-speed and sintered-metallic brake linings were "man-

1960 Corvair four-door sedan

1963 Corvair Monza convertible coupe

1961 Corvair Greenbrier Sports Wagon

1962 Corvair four-door wagon

1964 Corvair Monza Spyder coupe

1965 Corvair Monza convertible coupe

datory" options. The Spyder wasn't cheap—a minimum $2600—but it was the next best thing to a Porsche.

Corvair styling saw only minor changes through '64. Most occurred up front. The original winged Chevy bowtie gave way to a smaller emblem on a slim full-width chrome bar for '61. The '62s had simulated air intakes. A wide single chevron appeared for '63, then a double-bar version of the '61 trim. Aside from the aforementioned rear camber-compensator, the big news for '64 was a stroked 164-cid engine with 95 or 110 bhp in normally aspirated form. Spyder power was unchanged.

With 1965 came a design revolution. The sleek, second-generation Corvairs looked good even from normally un-flattering angles, a tribute to the work of GM Design under chief William L. Mitchell. It was something an Italian coachbuilder might do (as Pininfarina actually did, with a specially bodied '64 Corvair of generally similar lines)—nicely shaped and not overdone, with just the right amount of trim. Closed models were now pillarless hardtops, and a four-door returned to the 500 series.

The '65s were just as new under the skin. The turbo-six was up to 180 bhp, but the best all-around engine was the new 140-bhp version, standard for the top-line Corsa coupe and convertible, replacing Spyder. New cylinder heads, redesigned manifolds, and four progressively linked carburetors provided the extra power. This was an option

for lesser Corvairs, which continued with 95 bhp standard and 110 bhp at extra cost.

The 1960 Corvair had been the first mass-produced American car with a swing-axle rear suspension. The '65 was the first with fully independent suspension, not count-ing the '63 Corvette. The sole difference was that the Cor-vette linked its rear wheels with a single transverse leaf spring, while Corvair used individual coils. Both systems employed upper and lower control arms at each wheel. The uppers were actually the axle halfshafts; the lowers were unequal-length nonparallel trailing arms (two per side). Together, these controlled all lateral wheel motion. Small rubber-mounted rods extended from each lower arm to the main rear crossmember to absorb movement at the pivot points.

No question now about tricky behavior "at the limit": Corvair handling was nearly neutral, tending toward mild understeer at high speeds. The rear wheels, remaining at a constant angle with the ground, enabled the car to be pushed around corners with fine stability. Attention was also given to the front suspension, which was retuned to complement the new rear end and provide additional roll stiffness.

Like the Spyder in the first series, the 1965-66 Corsa is the most desirable second-generation Corvair. Base-priced at $2519 for the coupe and $2665 as a convertible, it came

1966 Corvair Corsa hardtop coupe

1967 Corvair Monza hardtop coupe

1968 Corvair Monza hardtop coupe

1969 Corvair Monza hardtop coupe

with full instrumentation, special exterior trim (including an aluminum rear panel for instant identification), deluxe interior and the 140-bhp engine. The turbo six, a $158 option, put it squarely in the performance league: less than 11 seconds 0-60 mph, the standing quarter-mile in 18 seconds at 80 mph. Given enough room, the Corsa could hit 115 mph yet would return more than 20 miles per gallon at moderate speeds.

Unfortunately, Corsa didn't sell particularly well against Ford's Mustang, which had been introduced about six months before and could better its performance. More critical was a decline in Monza sales. Though the most popular Corvair rallied slightly for '65, production plunged by some two-thirds the following year. Nader and his book were undoubtedly affecting sales, but Corvair's fate had already been sealed by an April 1965 GM directive that said in effect, "no more development work. Do only enough to meet federal requirements."

When Chevy's true Mustang-fighter, the Camaro, arrived for 1967, the Corvair line was trimmed to just 500 sedan and coupe, and Monza sedan, coupe, and convertible. The turbo engine was scratched, too. This was the last year for the hardtop sedans; all collector's items today.

The 1968-69 Corvairs were the rarest of the breed, available in just three models: 500 and Monza hardtops, and Monza convertible. They're readily distinguished by front side marker lights—clear lenses on the '68s, amber ones for '69. Monza convertibles were the scarcest of all: just 1386 and 521, respectively, for 1968-69.

With the lack of change and sales falling fast, it was obvious by 1968 that the Corvair was terminal, so many were surprised that Chevy even bothered with '69 models. Some dealers wouldn't sell them and others refused to service them, so the division offered what few buyers remained a $150 credit on the purchase of another Chevy through 1974. With that, the Corvair was finished.

In retrospect, the rear-engine Chevy died an undeserved death. Had it not been for the Monza, we might not have seen the Mustang—and ultimately, the Camaro. Left stillborn by GM's no-more-development edict was project XP-849, which progressed at least as far as a pair of clay mockups, one apparently a rear-engine design, the other with front drive. Intriguingly, both were badged "Corvair 2." A possible prelude to the unfortunate 1971 Chevy Vega but more likely for overseas consumption, XP-849 never materialized in these forms. But it showed that at least some GMers hadn't forgotten the adventuresome spirit of the original Corvair, despite corporate miscues and years of public controversy.

CORVAIR AT A GLANCE, 1960-1969										
	1960	1961	1962	1963	1964	1965	1966	1967	1968	1969
Price Range, $	1984-2238	1920-2331	1992-2846	1992-2798	2000-2811	2066-2665	2083-2662	2128-2540	2243-2626	2258-2641
Weight Range, lbs.	2270-2315	2320-2555	2350-2625	2330-2525	2365-2580	2385-2710	2400-2720	2435-2695	2470-2725	2515-2770
Wheelbases, in.	108	108	108	108	108	108	108	108	108	108
6 Cyl. Engines, hp	80-95	80-98	80-150	80-150	95-150	95-180	95-180	95-140	95-140	95-140

CHEVROLET CORVETTE

Born in 1953 as a production-ready Motorama exercise, America's most enduring sports car almost expired for lack of sales in 1955, the year Chevrolet bowed its milestone small-block V-8. But that engine combined with deft new styling to make Corvette a more serious—and salable—sports car for 1956. It became even more so for '57, thanks in part to optional "Ramjet" fuel injection on a V-8 enlarged from 265 to 283 cubic inches.

The third-generation Corvette announced for 1958 was longer, heavier, and gaudier on an unchanged 102-inch wheelbase. But it remained blindingly fast and was in some ways more practical than its predecessors. Despite only modest changes, sales continued upward through 1960, when Corvette exceeded the 10,000-unit level for the first time, thus assuring it a permanent place in the Chevy line. Featured for 1960 were a new aluminum clutch housing, radiator, and on fuel-injected engines, cylinder heads (though the last proved troublesome and were soon withdrawn). Also new were standard anti-sway bars front and rear, which greatly improved ride and handling and marked the first use of a rear sway bar on an American car.

Corvette achieved international recognition during 1960 with a fine showing in the arduous 24-hour of Le Mans in France. The three cars entered in the GT class by American sportsman Briggs Cunningham performed exceptionally well, one clocking 151 miles an hour down the long Mulsanne Straight. The highest placing Corvette ran eighth overall in the world's toughest endurance contest.

The 1960 Corvette might have been the advanced "Q-model" that had been under development since 1957, with rear transaxle, all-independent suspension, and even in-board disc brakes. But this was deemed too complicated and costly, so the existing platform was continued while designers and engineers created a less radical successor. Meantime, William L. Mitchell had replaced Harley Earl as GM design chief, and he promptly gave new life to the old Corvette styling.

It appeared for 1961 with a "tail-lift" along the lines of Mitchell's late-Fifties Stingray racer, a flowing "ducktail" design that not only increased luggage space some 20 percent but mated handsomely with the 1958-60 frontal styling, which Mitchell simplified by substituting mesh for the familiar chrome grille "teeth." Powerteams again stood pat, but there were more refinements: standard sunvisors, higher-capacity radiator, side-mount expansion tanks, and a wider choice of axle ratios. Base price stood at $3934, but that dough purchased a lot of go. Even the mildest 283 with Powerglide automatic was good for 7.7 seconds 0-60 mph and nearly 110 mph flat out; with the top 315-horsepower "fuelie" option and four-speed manual, it was 5.5 seconds and 130-plus mph. In case anyone doubted its prowess, a near-stock '61 finished 11th in the Sebring 12 Hours against far costlier and more exotic machinery.

Refinement was again the keynote for '62, but Chevy hinted at things to come by offering the next Corvette's engines in this last "traditional" model. There were four in all, one fuelie and three with carburetors, all 283s bored and stroked to 327 cid and delivering from 250 to a thumping 360 bhp. The fuel-injection system was modified, a new 3.08:1 final-drive ratio gave quieter cruising with the two lowest engines, and a heavy-duty suspension option returned from '59. Styling was cleaner than ever. Mitchell

1960 Corvette convertible roadster

1961 Corvette convertible roadster

1962 Corvette convertible roadster

1963 Corvette Sting Ray coupe

1963 Corvette Sting Ray convertible roadster

eliminated the chrome outline around the bodyside "cove" indentations and their optional two-toning, blacked in the grille, and added ribbed aluminum appliqués to rocker panels and the dummy reverse front-fender scoops. Corvette continued its winning ways in '62. Dr. Dick Thompson, the "flying dentist," won the national A-Production crown in SCCA, Don Yenko the B-Production title. More important to Chevy, sales kept climbing, reaching over 14,500.

For 1963 came the all-new Sting Ray, the first complete revision of Chevrolet's sports car in 10 years. The only things retained from previous Corvettes were four wheels, two seats, front suspension, the 327 V-8s, and fiberglass bodywork. Everything else was changed—and for the better.

It began with a slight reduction in overall length, a two-inch narrower rear track and a wheelbase pared four inches (to 98). Curb weight was also reduced, thanks to a new ladder-type box frame (replacing the heavy old X-member affair) and despite a new steel-reinforced "cage" that made for a stronger, safer cockpit. In fact, the Sting Ray had almost twice as much steel support in its main body structure compared to earlier Corvettes, and less fiberglass in its body. Brakes remained drums but were now self-adjusting, and the fronts were wider.

The big news was independent rear suspension, a first for a modern U.S. production car. Devised by Corvette engineer Zora Arkus-Duntov, it comprised a frame-mounted differential with U-jointed halfshafts acting on a single transverse leaf spring; differential-mounted control arms ran laterally and slightly forward to the hub carriers in order to limit fore/aft movement, with a pair of trailing radius rods behind. It was elegantly simple, relatively cheap, and highly effective. Just as nice, front/rear weight distribution improved to 48/52 percent from 53/47. With all this, Corvette ride and handling were better than ever.

Engines were unchanged save alternators to replace generators, plus positive crankcase ventilation and smaller flywheels. Competition options included stiff suspension, metallic brake linings, handsome cast-aluminum knock-off wheels, and a 36.5-gallon long-distance fuel tank.

Sting Ray styling was dramatic, evolved since 1959 from both the Q-model and Mitchell's Stingray racer. The customary convertible roadster gained a sleek fastback coupe companion whose curved rear window was vertically split by a body-color "spine." Duntov lobbied against this, saying it hampered outward vision. Mitchell huffed that "if you take that off you might as well forget the whole thing." Duntov ultimately won, and a one-piece backlight was substituted after '63, leaving the "split-window coupe" a one-year model—and highly prized because of it.

Shared highlights comprised hidden headlights (in rotating pods that blended with the pointy nose when the lamps were off), an attractive beltline dip, humped fenders, slim L-shape half-bumpers at each end, a continuation of the 1961-62 "ducktail," and a sharp full-perimeter "character line" at mid-body. A new "dual cockpit" dashboard was a fresh approach that worked remarkably well. Doors cut into the roof facilitated cockpit access on the coupe, and interior space was at least as good as in previous Corvettes

1964 Corvette Sting Ray coupe

1965 Corvette Sting Ray coupe

1966 Corvette Sting Ray convertible roadster

despite the shorter wheelbase. A lift-off hardtop remained optional for the roadster. Interestingly, a four-seat coupe was considered, progressing as far as a complete full-size mockup, but was rejected as being out of character for Corvette. Sting Ray production prototypes were extensively evaluated in the wind tunnel, an unusual practice that reduced frontal area by a square foot.

The Sting Ray quickly proved the fastest and most road-able 'Vette yet—and the most popular: 1963 sales were nearly twice the record '62 total, about 10,000 for each body style. Performance had less to do with this than the wider market appeal of new extra-cost creature comforts: leather upholstery, power steering, power brakes (at last), AM/FM radio, and air conditioning, to name a few.

Over the next four years, the Sting Ray was progressively cleaned up, Chevy removing what little nonsense there was or making it functional, as with the fake hood louvers and coupe rear quarter vents for '64. The following year, the sculptured hood was smoothed out and the front-fender slots opened up. The design was virtually perfect by 1967, the only changes being a single oblong backup light above the license plate, bolt-on instead of knock-off aluminum wheels, revised front fender louvers, and, more dubious, an optional vinyl covering for the roadster hardtop.

Of course, there were important technical improvements in these years. The fuelie 327 delivered up to 375 bhp for 1964, while '65 brought optional four-wheel disc

brakes (for stopping power to match the steadily escalating performance) and Corvette's first big-block V-8, the 396-cid, 425-bhp "Mark IV." The last became a 427 for '66 and beyond. To handle its brute force, Chevy fitted stiffer suspension, super-duty clutch, and a larger radiator and fan. With 4.11:1 rear axle, a '66 Mark IV could do 0-60 mph in less than five seconds and more than 140 mph—terrific for a civilized, fully equipped machine costing around $4500. The small-block "fuelie" was dropped in 1965 due to high production costs and low sales.

But Corvette sales as a whole set new records in all but one of the Sting Ray years, peaking at nearly 28,000 for 1966. Horsepower seemed to set yearly records, too. That peak was reached with 1967's stupendous L88, an aluminum-head 427 with 12.5:1 compression, wild cam, and big four-barrel carb rated at no less than 560 bhp. Only 20 cars were so equipped, but they were symbolic of how far the 'Vette had come.

Many high-power Sting Rays naturally went racing, though they often bowed to Carroll Shelby's stark, super-quick Cobras. But there were bright spots. Don Yenko was SCCA national B-Production champ in 1963, a Roger Penske car won its class at Nassau '65, and 1966 saw Sting Rays place 12th overall in the Daytona Continental and 9th at Sebring.

The Sting Ray was a tough act to follow, and not everyone liked its 1968 follow-up. Arriving for the first year of

1967 Corvette Sting Ray coupe

1967 Corvette Sting Ray convertible roadster

1968 Corvette convertible roadster

1969 Corvette Stingray coupe

federal safety and emissions standards, it combined a new seven-inch-longer body (most of the increase in front overhang) with essentially carryover engines and chassis. Styling, previewed by the 1965 Mako Shark II show car, was all humpy and muscular, with bulging fenders housing seven-inch-wide wheels for better roadholding. Flip-up headlamps and modest "lip" spoilers at each end were also featured, but, like the Sting Ray, there was still no opening trunklid. And the name wasn't Sting Ray anymore, just Corvette. Coupe and convertible returned, the former a new notchback style with an innovative "T-top" whose twin panels could be removed to create a semi-convertible. Mechanical changes were limited to standardizing the previously optional all-disc brakes and substituting General Motors' fine three-speed Turbo Hydra-Matic for the archaic Powerglide as the automatic option.

This fifth-generation Corvette would have bowed for 1967 had engineer Duntov not held it up to work out some kinks. Yet the '68s had plenty of problems. The most glaring was poor workmanship, but the new design was also judged needlessly gimmicky, having a trouble-prone pop-up cowl panel hiding the wipers and a dashboard awash with winking lights. The narrower cockpit (a penalty of the new wasp-waisted styling), reduced luggage space, and 150-pound gain in curb weight won no friends—nor did inadequate cooling on big-block cars. Yet despite all this, the '68 set another Corvette sales record: more than 28,500 units.

The tally was nearly 38,800 for '69, when the Stingray name returned (as one word). Duntov did his best to fix flaws, finding a little more cockpit space (smaller steering wheel, slimmer door panels), adding an override so the wiper panel could be left up in freezing weather, and so on. Detail styling changes comprised neater exterior door handles, black instead of chrome grille bars, and backup lights integrated with the inner taillights. Handling improved via wider wheels and a stiffer frame. Emissions considerations prompted lower compression ratios and a small-block stroked to 350 cid, while a fourth 427 option appeared with 430 bhp and available axle ratios from 2.75:1 to 4.56:1. Even wilder was the all-aluminum ZL-1 big-block, a virtual Can-Am racing engine priced at a formidable $3000. Production? Just two.

While Sting Rays are the most coveted Sixties Corvettes, any member of the three design generations that span this decade is now a prime collectible automobile. And why not? Through them all, Corvette remained "America's only true sports car." As Car Life said of the '68: "Corvettes are for driving, by drivers. The Corvette driver will be tired of smiling long before he's tired of the car."

CORVETTE AT A GLANCE, 1960-1969										
	1960	1961	1962	1963	1964	1965	1966	1967	1968	1969
Price Range, $	3872	3934	4038	4037-4252	4037-4252	4106-4321	4084-4295	4141-4353	4320-4663	4438-4781
Weight Range, lbs.	2840	2905	2925	2859-2881	2945-2960	2975-2985	2985-3005	3000-3020	3055-3065	3140-3145
Wheelbases, in.	102	102	102	98	98	98	98	98	98	98
8 Cyl. Engines, hp	230-315	230-315	250-360	250-360	250-375	250-425	300-425	300-435	300-435	300-435

CHRYSLER

Chrysler entered the Sixties with repeated declarations that there would never be a small Chrysler—though there would be when the time was right and the government would allow little else. Let Buick, Olds, and Pontiac rush to compacts. Dodge and Plymouth would field—and sometimes suffer with—smaller cars; Chryslers would continue to be big, brawny, and luxurious. And so they were, right through to the mid-Seventies.

The 1960-61 models were the last of the outlandishly finned Exner-styled Chryslers that the division had prospered with in the mid-Fifties, then suffered with as the decade wound to a close. They were also the first Chryslers to employ unit construction instead of the traditional body-on-frame. Since "unibodies" were held together by welds rather than nuts and bolts, they weren't as prone to rattles and looseness, though they were more susceptible to rust. Stylewise, the 1960 Chryslers were fairly sparing in their use of chrome, sporting 300-style inverted-trapezoid grilles and lots of glass. A new option that year was swiveling front seats that pivoted outward through an automatic latch release when a door was opened, a feature first seen on the 300E and other '59 Chrysler products.

Wheelbases and series were unchanged from '59, as were Chrysler's two big wedgehead V-8s. The low-line Windsor and mid-range Saratoga (the latter in its final year) packed a 383 with 305/325 horsepower. A big-bore 413 gave 350 bhp in New Yorkers, which comprised a convertible, two hardtops, a four-door sedan, and two Town & Country wagons. Prices ran from $4409 to $5131, putting New Yorkers just under Imperial and about even with the senior Buicks. Sales were good but hardly great: about 20,000 per year for 1960-61.

As ever, the limited-edition 300 was the most exciting Chrysler. The sixth-edition 1960 F-model continued the tradition with special racy styling touches, an exclusive new four-place bucket-seat interior, road-hugging suspension—still with Chrysler's much-ballyhooed torsion-bar springing in front—and a newly optional French-made Pont-a-Mousson four-speed gearbox. A set of ram-induction manifolds lifted its 413 V-8 to 375 standard horses or 400 optional, good for a standing quarter-mile of 16 seconds at 85 mph. The F rode hard, but cornered better than any other car of its size. A half-dozen different axle ratios were available. Andy Granatelli combined the 3.03 gearset with a tuned engine and some streamlined body modifications to approach 190 mph in a flying-mile run. At $5411 for the hardtop and $5811 for the convertible, the 300F wasn't cheap, but it offered a lot for the money.

The '61 line was mostly a repeat of 1960 except for somewhat more contrived styling. Windsor, still on its 122-inch wheelbase, moved up to replace Saratoga, while the base series was renamed Newport and downpriced to as little as $2964 for the family four-door. With that, Newport quickly became Chrysler's volume line at prices that remained very competitive through 1964, a point emphasized in division advertising. By 1965, annual sales volume was above 125,000 units. The '61 carried a 265-bhp 361 V-8, while Windsor and New Yorker retained their previous engines. That year's 300G didn't offer the four-speed option like the 1960 F, but did return to 15-inch wheels for the first time on

1960 300F hardtop coupe

a "letter-series" Chrysler since 1956. Both ram-induction 413s continued at their previous power ratings.

Chrysler Corporation's fortunes were shaky in these years, but Chrysler Division actually improved both its volume and industry rank. After sinking to 12th on over 77,000 cars for 1960, it finished 11th on better than 96,000 units for '61.

Nevertheless, the company's general sales difficulties hastened a management shakeup that had an immediate effect on products. At the end of July 1961, a beleaguered "Tex" Colbert retired as president, a role he had resumed in 1960 when William Newberg quit the post after two months amid allegations of having financial interests in several Chrysler suppliers. The presidency was turned over to former administrative vice-president Lynn A. Townsend. When Townsend moved up to become board chairman in January 1967, he was succeeded by Virgil Boyd, who stayed on through early 1970. These changes also prompted Exner to depart late in '61 after shaping the '63 corporate line. His successor as company styling chief was Elwood Engel, recruited from Ford and generally credited for the elegant 1961 Lincoln Continental.

The mid-Sixties thus saw a new direction for Chrysler styling. For 1962, the division fielded what Exner called the "plucked chickens": a repeat of the '61 *sans* fins. The 1963-64s had what was billed as "the crisp, clean custom look"—chiseled but chunky. For 1965, Engel unveiled squarish but smooth bodies with fenders edged in bright metal, one of his trademarks.

Among the '62 "plucked chickens" was a four-model group of "non-letter" 300s: convertible, hardtop coupe, and four-doors with and without B-pillars powered by the same engine as the now-departed Windsor. All could be optioned with sporty features like center console and front bucket seats, and all save the pillared sedan (only 1801 built) were quite popular at prices in the $3300-$3800 range. But they hurt that year's 300H, which cost $1600-$1800 more yet looked almost the same. As a result, letter-series volume dropped from about 1530 for '61 to just 558.

For 1963-64, New Yorker switched from its customary 126-inch wheelbase to ride the 122-inch "junior" chassis. Despite shrinking to the same general size as less costly Chryslers, it sold strongly in both years. Arriving as 1963 "spring specials" were the 300 Pace Setter hardtop and convertible and the New Yorker Salon hardtop sedan. The former, commemorating Chrysler's selection as that year's Indianapolis 500 pace car, was identified by crossed check-ered-flag emblems and special trim. The Salon came with such standard luxuries as air conditioning; AM/FM radio; Auto Pilot speed control; power brakes, steering, seats, and windows; TorqueFlite automatic; color-keyed wheel covers, and vinyl roof. *Sans* Pace Setters, the same lineup returned for '64, with engines and styling both broadly the same.

The 1963-64 300J/300K (the letter "I" was skipped to avoid confusion with the number "1") were big, burly cars in the letter-series tradition. The J came only as a hardtop; the convertible 300 was reinstated with the K. Just 400 Js were built in all, a record low for Chrysler's limited edition, but the K saw a healthy 3600-plus. All ran 413s with 360/390 bhp, down slightly from 300H ratings. The 300L

1961 New Yorker convertible coupe

1961 New Yorker four-door hardtop

1962 New Yorker four-door hardtop

1962 300 hardtop coupe

1964 300 hardtop coupe

1963 300J hardtop coupe

1965 300L hardtop coupe

1964 New Yorker four-door sedan

1967 Newport Custom hardtop coupe

1966 New Yorker hardtop sedan

1967 New Yorker hardtop coupe

of 1965, which would be the last of the true letter-series cars, saw 2845 copies, including a mere 440 convertibles. None of these 300s were quite the stormers their predecessors had been, but they remained the most roadable Chryslers. Declining sales with the advent of the non-letter 300s is what killed them, no doubt.

Chrysler did very well for 1965, selling over 125,000 Newports, nearly 30,000 non-letter 300s and almost 50,000 New Yorkers. Things went even better for '66: Sales of the 300 nearly doubled, and Newport climbed by 42,000 units.

The post-1964 "Engel Chryslers" were shorter than their Exner forebears but just as roomy inside. Wheelbase was 124 inches for all models except wagons (121 through '66, then back to 122). Expanding the '67 line were Newport Custom two- and four-door hardtops and four-door sedans tagged some $200 above their base-series counterparts and accordingly promoted as "a giant step in luxury, a tiny step in price." Deluxe interiors were the big attraction. Upholstery was a combination of jacquard cloth and textured vinyl, and pull-down center armrests were included. Like other '67 Chryslers, the Custom dash was a gadget-lover's paradise, sprouting no fewer than eight toggle switches, three thumbwheels, 16 pushbuttons, three slid-

ing levers, and 12 other controls that, as Chrysler brochures proclaimed, "put you in charge of almost every option in the book." Vinyl-covered lift handles appeared on Custom trunklids, and there were "over 1000 chrome accents along the sides, plus 15 gold crown medallions," according to the brochure.

The luxurious New Yorker Town & Country wagon was dropped after 1965 (sales had been slow for years), but six- and nine-passenger Newport wagons continued through '68, after which T&C became a separate series. All typically came with full vinyl upholstery instead of the cloth-and-vinyl of Newport sedans. Standard equipment for wagons in these years included power steering, power brakes, and TorqueFlite automatic. Again typifying Chrysler's emphasis on "showroom appeal" was its wagons' three-in-one front seat. Though it looked like a conventional bench, it was split so that each half could be adjusted fore/aft independently. The seatback on the passenger's side could be reclined.

Spring 1968 brought an interesting $126 option called "Sportsgrain"—wagon-style simulated wood side paneling for the Newport convertible and hardtop coupe. It wasn't very popular, and was thus dropped after '68, so a Sports-

34

grain convertible must be rare indeed, as Chrysler built only 2847 ragtop Newports in all. Announced at the same time, but finding somewhat higher acceptance, were Newport Special two- and four-door hardtops with a turquoise color scheme, later extended to 300s.

Engine choices for '65 included 270- and 315-bhp 383s for Newport and 300, and a 413 with 340 or 360 bhp for New Yorkers and 300L. The more potent 383 gained 10 horses for '66, when a huge new 440 big-block arrived as standard New Yorker power, rated at 350 bhp. This became standard 300 fare for 1967, when New Yorkers were bumped up to 375 bhp. The 440s stood pat for 1968-69, but the 383s were retuned to 290 and 330 bhp, this despite the advent of federal emissions standards.

All these moves, especially the more conservative Engel styling, paid off in vastly higher volume: 206,000-plus for '65 and nearly 265,000 for '66. Though sales dipped to only 219,000 for '67, Chrysler ran 10th in industry output in each of these years, then claimed ninth with 1968 production that just topped the '66 record.

The all-new "fuselage-styled" '69s sold almost as well. If not the most beautiful Chryslers of the decade, they were at least handsome with their big loop-type bumper/grille combinations, bulbous bodysides, and low rooflines. Both Newport series were brought up to the 124-inch chassis, and all models were bigger than ever: almost 225 inches long and nearly 80 inches wide—about as big as an American car would get.

Big changes were evident in Chrysler as a company by 1969. On the manufacturing side, fit-and-finish, which had been mediocre at best since 1957, had become a major priority, though engineers still struggled against their cars' reputation for poor body durability. On the administrative side, the old centralized corporate structure, which had been decentralized under Colbert, was recentralized under Townsend, who also moved to provide greater divisional identity between Chrysler-Plymouth and Dodge.

But Chrysler, both as a make and as a company, would face tough sledding in the Seventies, hampered by too many gas guzzlers in the aftermath of a sudden fuel shortage, plus quality control that wasn't improved nearly as much as it needed to be. These and other factors conspired to put Chrysler on the ropes by 1979—but that, as they say, is another story.

1968 300 convertible coupe

CHRYSLER AT A GLANCE, 1960-1969										
	1960	**1961**	**1962**	**1963**	**1964**	**1965**	**1966**	**1967**	**1968**	**1969**
Price Range, $	3194-5841	2964-5841	2964-5461	2964-5860	2901-5860	3009-4935	3052-4233	3159-4339	3306-4500	3414-4615
Weight Range, lbs.	3815-4535	3690-4455	3690-4445	3760-4370	3760-4395	4000-4745	3875-4550	3920-4550	3840-4410	3891-4485
Wheelbases, in.	122-126	122-126	122-126	122	122	121-124	121-124	122-124	122-124	122-124
8 Cyl. Engines, hp	305-400	265-400	265-405	265-390	265-390	270-360	270-350	270-375	290-375	290-375

DESOTO

The American auto industry recorded its third death in as many years when DeSoto was discontinued in late 1960 after a token run of 1961 models and 33 years as Chrysler Corporation's "in-between" medium-price make. The end came only some 13 months after the demise of Ford Motor Company's newer, much shorter-lived Edsel (see entry), and for much the same reason: the decline of the medium-price market brought on by the 1958 recession. But DeSoto was in trouble well before that time. In fact, one writer termed it "excess baggage" almost from the start.

Of course, this was hardly the original plan. Introduced for 1929, DeSoto was designed to bridge the price gap between Plymouth and Dodge and thus complete the General Motors-like "stairstep" model hierarchy that Chrysler had been evolving. By the late Thirties, DeSoto had been upgraded into a sort of junior Chrysler, priced slightly higher than Dodge. There was nothing wrong with that, of course, and sales were good, if not spectacular, up to World War II. DeSoto continued doing well in the early postwar years. But by the late Fifties, it had been all but crowded out of its market slot from both above and below, a situation not unlike Cadillac's LaSalle in the early Forties.

This reflected a change in Chrysler's marketing approach for 1955. Before, the firm had maintained three dual-franchise dealer networks: Chrysler-Plymouth, DeSoto-Plymouth, and Dodge-Plymouth. Pairing the low-price make with each of the company's medium-price brands not only made sense but had been Chrysler's salvation during the Airflow disaster of the Depression-era Thirties. But when Imperial was spun off from Chrysler as a separate make for '55 (see entry), Chrysler Division began concentrating on the lower end of its price spectrum, thus interfering with the upper end of the DeSoto line. Dodge, meantime, began an ambitious move upmarket with larger and more luxurious cars that ate into sales of the lower-price DeSotos. Then came the '58 recession, and the firm consolidated from five divisions to two: Dodge and Chrysler-DeSoto-Plymouth (the latter absorbing an interim Imperial Division). With that and sharply lower sales, rumors of DeSoto's imminent demise were abroad by early the following year, which only accelerated the slide.

The statistics were indeed ominous. Though calendar production was up slightly over '58, DeSoto's 1959 model-year volume dropped nearly 4000 units, and its output in both years was less than half that of 1957's total (some

1960 Adventurer hardtop coupe

1960 Adventurer hardtop coupe

1961 hardtop coupe

117,500), which would prove to be the make's last really good showing. DeSoto, of course, was in the same kind of trouble as its medium-price rivals, including Oldsmobile, Buick, and Mercury. But those makes were generating higher volume and could thus stand to lose more sales. Moreover, all were readying compacts for 1961 that promised to make up for diminished big-car demand. While forward planning did envision downsized standard DeSotos for 1962, there was no compact in the works—other than the forthcoming 1960 Valiant, which was logically assigned to bread-and-butter Plymouth.

At first, Chrysler strongly denied that DeSoto was about to be dropped, and even staged a 1959 celebration to mark the make's 30th anniversary and production of the two-millionth DeSoto. Press releases noted that almost a million DeSotos were still registered, and the division announced that $25 million had been earmarked for future models, with $7 million for 1960 alone. Officials also noted that tooling commitments had been made for 1961, and that work toward 1962-63 was underway. Finally, Chrysler pointed out that DeSoto had regularly made a profit.

But the public didn't buy any of this in 1960. Valiant sold very well and Plymouth did fairly well, but DeSoto sales in the first two months of the year came to only 4746, a mere 0.51 percent of the industry total—even less than the comparable '59 figures of 6134 and 0.72 percent. By the end of 1960, plans for a restyled '62 DeSoto had been shelved, and the '61 models, announced in October, were withdrawn. DeSoto-Plymouth dealers then became Chrysler-Plymouth stores—to the chagrin of existing C-P dealers nearby.

Signs of distress were as close as the 1960 sales catalog, where offerings were reduced appreciably. From four series for 1957-59, ranging from the low-priced Dodge-based Firesweep to the high-performance Adventurer, the range thinned to just six models in two series, each offering sedan, hardtop sedan, and two-door hardtop. Adventurer was now the upper line, though it was priced a few hundred dollars less than the '59 Fireflite. Fireflite, in turn, moved down into the $3000 region previously occupied by Firesweep and Firedome. Station wagons and convertibles were dropped. Perhaps not surprisingly, the most popular 1960 DeSotos were sedans: the Fireflite with 9032 copies, the Adventurer with 5746. Four-door hardtops were the least popular: 1958 and 2759, respectively. Comparable hardtop coupes numbered 3494 and 3092.

All 1960 DeSotos rode a 122-inch wheelbase shared with Chrysler and Dodge, and employed the corporation's much-ballyhooed new "unibody" construction (body and frame welded into a single unit)—though that was hardly a new idea, even at Chrysler. Adventurers were powered by the corporate 383-cubic-inch V-8, tuned for 305 horsepower as in the low-line Chrysler Windsor. Fireflites carried a 295-bhp 361 as used in mid-range Dodges. Chrysler's superb three-speed TorqueFlite automatic transmission with pushbutton control was standard for Adventurers. The TorqueFlite and two-speed PowerFlite automatics were optional for FireFlites. Styling was very similar to Chrysler's, distinguished mainly by a busier grille insert and gaudier taillights. Fins were about as high as they'd ever be on a Chrysler product, but the overall

1961 hardtop sedan

package looked pretty good—burly and serious. The same could not be said for performance. An Adventurer could stay with a Chrysler Windsor, but would lose to the more potent 383 Saratoga or a Dodge Phoenix, the latter being somewhat smaller and lighter.

Like Edsel, DeSoto made a half-hearted last-gasp effort, only its '61 offerings were fewer in number—just a pair of hardtops without a series name—and didn't look as nice. Division publicists extolled styling "individuality," but these cars were generally considered ugly with their diagonally stacked quad headlights, heavy-handed rear-end treatment, and a clumsy double grille comprising a lattice-like lower section and a large blunt oval displaying stylized block letters on a mesh background.

After 2123 hardtop sedans and just 911 hardtop coupes, all built before Christmas 1960, DeSoto production was quietly phased out and existing orders were filled mostly with Chrysler Windsors. It was a sad finale for a make that had won Chrysler considerable prestige and profits for more than three decades.

Yet, ironically, the end actually came too soon. Less than a year later, the '61 DeSoto was effectively resurrected at Dodge to bolster that division's slow-selling 1962 standards, which had been reduced to near-compact size. Called Custom 880, this reborn big Dodge was much like the last DeSoto, and even cost about the same, but sold much better, thanks to smoother styling and more model choices.

So in retrospect, DeSoto's rapid decline, like Edsel's, likely stemmed as much from a "loser" image as a difficult medium-price market. That, when coupled with cowardly "bean-counters" and unsympathetic product planners who were only too eager to finish the job, was sufficient to bring about the DeSoto's demise.

DESOTO AT A GLANCE, 1960-1961		
	1960	1961
Price Range, $	3017-3727	3102-3167
Weight Range, lbs.	3865-3945	3760-3820
Wheelbases, in.	122	122
8 Cyl. Engines, hp	295-330	265

DODGE

Dodge, like Chevrolet, turned from dependable but dull cars to high-flying performance in 1955. The Sixties would see Chrysler Corporation's second-best-selling make strengthen its position in the "hot car" field, even while pushing upward into what had been DeSoto price territory and diversifying with low-cost compacts and intermediates. Volume rose rapidly after 1964 to an annual average of over a half-million units. The peak came for 1966: a record 633,000. But competitors moved up, too, so Dodge's standing in the production race was fifth or sixth in its best years and eighth or ninth in troubled 1961-63.

Responding to the growing market for more sensible cars evident in the late Fifties, Dodge fielded a much broader 1960 lineup divided into "junior" and "senior" groups. The former was the new Dart, sixes and V-8s on a 118-inch wheelbase for all models save wagons, which rode a 122. There were three series: Seneca, Pioneer, and Phoenix in ascending order of price and plush. Phoenix offered a convertible, hardtop coupe and sedan, and pillared four-door, while the lesser lines were limited to wagons, two- and four-door sedans, and a Pioneer two-door hardtop. Big Dodges comprised V-8 Matadors and Polaras on the 122-inch wheelbase. All employed unit body/chassis construction, new at Chrysler Corporation that year (though actually revived from the abortive Thirties Airflow) and bore more sculptured styling announced by bright, blunt, and busy front ends. Fins were still in evidence, ending well ahead of pod-like taillights on Matador/Polara, near the rear of more conventional fenders on Darts.

Despite appearances, most '60 Dodges were relatively light and offered good performance with reasonable economy. That was especially true of base-engine models, which carried the larger, 225-cid version of that year's new Chrysler Corporation slant six. Initially rated at 145 horsepower, this durable workhorse would carry on into the early Eighties. Dart's V-8 was the solid, reliable 318 with 230/255 bhp. Matadors used the 295-bhp Chrysler 361,

optional on Dart Pioneer and Phoenix. Polaras packed a 383 (available for Phoenix and Matador) with 325/330 bhp. After a lackluster '59, Dodge scored impressively higher sales for 1960: up over 200,000 for the model year to nearly 368,000, good for a sixth on the industry production roster, up two spots.

Per long-established practice, the 1961 line included a Dodge version of a Plymouth product: the 106.5-inch-wheelbase Valiant compact that had bowed the previous year. Called Lancer, it shared the Valiant's "unibody" structure and basic styling but stood apart with a horizontal-bar grille and slightly better trim. Also like Valiant, there were two Lancer series, called 170 and 770, each with two-door sedan, four-door sedan, and four-door wagon. The 770 also included a hardtop coupe, new to Valiant for '61, as was the pillared two-door. Power came from the smaller, 170-cid slant six with 101 bhp. The Dart's 225 engine was optional.

The Dart itself was substantially facelifted for '61, sporting a deeply concave full-width grille incorporating quad headlamps, plus curious reverse-slant tailfins. The senior Matador was dropped and remaining Polara models were restyled to be Dart dead-ringers. Engines choices, for the most part, were the same as those in 1960. Among these was Dodge's customary D 500 option, in those days a 383 with twin four-barrel carburetors and ram-induction manifolding, good for 330 bhp. In a Dart, that translated to about 10 pounds for each bhp, a super power-to-weight ratio that meant 120-mph flat out and acceleration to match. Torsion-bar suspension and oversized Chrysler brakes made it as roadable as it was quick. It was even quicker when stuffed full of Chrysler 413, a ram-induction wedgehead delivering 350 or 375 bhp as a new Dart option, though price was high and availability quite limited.

Alas, Dodge sales dropped by over 25 percent for '61, reflecting increased competition and an overall industry downtrend. Lancer didn't sell well, but it was a stopgap

1960 Polara hardtop sedan (*left front*), Dart Phoenix hardtop sedan (*right front*), Matador hardtop coupe (*left rear*), and Dart Pioneer wagon (*right rear*).

anyway. A successor was in the works, so it returned for '62 with a busier grille and a smart bucket-seat GT hardtop (replacing the 770 model) as its only significant changes.

Meantime, brand-new Darts in base, 330, and 440 series arrived on a 116-inch wheelbase, measuring six inches shorter overall and weighing 400 pounds less than their '61 counterparts. Above them was a sporty bucket-seat Polara 500 group offering hardtops with two and four doors, plus a convertible. Chrysler styling chief Virgil Exner thought that if Americans liked compacts, they'd go for downsized "standard" cars, too. But the designer was about 15 years ahead of his time, and, aggravated by frankly odd Valiant-like looks, these cars sold as poorly as the Lancer.

But performance fans roundly applauded the smaller, lighter Darts, mainly because the big-block 413 returned with even more muscle and in three versions: 365, 380, 410, and a rollicking 420 bhp. Shoehorned into the lightest 330 two-doors, these cars began terrorizing the nation's dragstrips, thus burnishing what remained of Dodge's somewhat tarnished performance reputation from the Fifties and setting the stage for even wilder things to come. In fact, big-inch Dodge intermediates won the National Hot Rod Association Championship in 1962 and would reign supreme for the next few years on literally every quarter-mile. They were also strong contenders at Daytona.

But performance alone doesn't necessarily sell cars, and Dodge's total 1962 volume sank to about 240,500, off some 30,000 units in a year when most rivals scored higher sales. Things would have been even worse had it not been for the Chrysler-based large cars introduced at mid-year as the Custom 880. Effectively taking over for DeSoto in the corporate lineup, they looked like the finless '61 Polaras they were, with '62 Chrysler-style "plucked chicken" tails and a 265-bhp 361 V-8.

While Plymouth struggled on for another year with downsized "standards," Dodge increased wheelbase to 119 inches and pushed performance even harder. What had been the Dart was now just "Dodge," with base-trim models omitted. Styling became cleaner and more conventional, though the front end was still somewhat odd. Though engines remained broadly the same, a bore job took the 413 wedge to 426 cubes and 370/375 bhp. But the big news was the "Ramcharger," a super-performance 426 with aluminum pistons and high-lift cam punching out 415/425 bhp.

Dodge did field a Dart for '63, but it was a very different car: mostly new replacement for the compact Lancer. (The name change was a last-minute decision.) Actually, it was that year's redesigned Valiant with more crisply styled exterior sheetmetal and five extra inches in wheelbase (111 total except wagons, still at 106). Sedans and wagons made up the 170 and 270 series, with convertibles offered in 270 and bucket-seat GT guise, plus a GT hardtop coupe. At the other end of the scale, Custom 880s returned with lower-priced 880 companions, all identified by revised grilles with fine vertical bars. With so much new, Dodge surged past Rambler to grab seventh in the industry standings on record volume of over 446,000 units.

The 1964 lineup was much like '63's, with facelifts that continued Dodge's move back to more orthodox looks.

1961 Polara convertible coupe

1961 Polara hardtop sedan

1962 Polara 500 hardtop coupe

1962 Dart two-door sedan

1963 440 four-door sedan

1963 Polara 500 hardtop coupe

1964 440 hardtop coupe

1965 Custom 880 convertible coupe

1965 Coronet 500 convertible coupe

1965 Dart GT convertible coupe

Darts became livelier, as Valiant's new 273-cid small-block V-8 was added to the options list, bringing 180 bhp. That year's Ramcharger was Chrysler's fabled hemi-head V-8, returning to the performance wars in a new 426 version with 425 bhp—but only for racing. The top showroom power options remained 426 wedgeheads, now with 365 bhp standard or 415 with high-compression heads. But hemi-powered Dodge/Plymouth intermediates provided plenty of entertainment anyway, dominating the '64 NASCAR season beginning with a 1-2-3 sweep at the Daytona 500. In the production race, Dodge swept back into sixth for the first time since 1960.

For 1965, the Coronet name returned for the first time since 1959 on a revamped mid-size line with more square-cut styling and a 117-inch wheelbase for all models save wagons (116 inches). Offerings comprised six and V-8 base-trim sedans and wagons, the same plus convertibles and hardtop coupes in 440 trim, and a pair of bucket-seat 500s. A much-altered 115-inch-wheelbase Coronet Hemi-Charger two-door sedan weighing just 3165 pounds was offered, but only for off-road drag racing. Base-priced at $3165, it came with heavy-duty springs and shocks, anti-roll bar, four-speed transmission, and strong "police" brakes. Performance was more than ample: 0-60 mph in seven seconds. "Civilians" contented themselves with the more civilized new buckets-and console Coronet 500 hardtop and convertible. Darts again sported a mild facelift.

Capping the '65 line was a completely new group of 121-inch wheelbase Polaras and Custom 880s, plus a companion sports/luxury hardtop, the $3355 Monaco. All shared chassis and body structure with that year's larger, redesigned Chryslers, including a new conservatively square basic shape drawn by the recently recruited Elwood Engel, differentiated mainly by a "dumbbell" grille and delta taillamps.

Dart was again modestly restyled for '66, while Coronet returned in standard, Deluxe, 440, and 500 series, the last newly expanded with a four-door sedan. All sported curvier rear fenders, a bolder grille, and wedgy taillights. Custom 880 was renamed Monaco, and the big bucket-seat job became a Monaco 500. These, along with the Polaras, got wider taillights and crisper lower-body contours, plus Chrysler's new big-block 440 V-8 with 350 bhp as their top power option.

A bright new addition was the Charger, essentially a Coronet hardtop coupe with fastback roofline, hidden headlamps, and a sporty interior featuring full-length center console and individual fold-down rear bucket seats. A 318 was standard, but other V-8s were available—including the 426 hemi, now a regular production option for all Chrysler intermediates. Also listed were manual transmission, "Rallye" suspension, and a long list of luxury extras. A 383 Charger with TorqueFlite could run 0-60 mph in about nine seconds and hit 110 mph.

In all, 1966 was a great Dodge year. After easing to 489,000 units for '65, volume shot up to its aforementioned decade high of 633,000, good for fifth in Detroit production. Dodge wouldn't rank so high again until '88.

For 1967, the Dart got an all-new unit structure on the existing wheelbase and lost its wagons. Polara/Monaco

1966 Coronet 500 hardtop coupe

1966 Polara hardtop sedan

1967 Polara convertible coupe

1968 Coronet 500 convertible coupe

1968 Dart GTS hardtop coupe

1966 Charger hardtop coupe

1967 Coronet R/T hardtop coupe

1967 Dart GT hardtop coupe

1968 Charger R/T hardtop coupe

1968 Monaco 500 hardtop coupe

also got a new structure: a full-size body/frame platform shared with Chrysler and the Plymouth Fury. Styling was somewhat more contrived, lower and sleeker but with rear decks longer than hoods and a complex grille comprising a square vertical-bar section between openings split by horizontal bars. Charger retained its 1966 look, and a belated facelift gave Coronets a similar appearance.

Continuing its performance push, Dodge issued a sportier Coronet for '67. Called R/T (for "Road/Track"), it came as a convertible and hardtop coupe with standard 375-bhp 440 "Magnum" V-8, heavy-duty suspension, wide tires, and oversize brakes—Dodge's entry in the burgeoning muscle-car market uncovered by Pontiac's GTO. A similar package was devised for a new Charger R/T. The 426 hemi remained optional for intermediates, still on a limited basis. Despite this appealing lineup, Dodge fell back

1969 Charger 500 hardtop coupe

1969 Charger Daytona hardtop coupe

1969 Coronet R/T hardtop coupe

1969 Polara 500 hardtop coupe

to seventh place on model-year volume of nearly 466,000 units.

Predictably, 1968 brought a facelifted Dart and full-size Dodges, as it was time for Coronet and Charger to be fully revised. They were the best-looking mid-size Dodges yet: long and low, with rounded "fuselages" and pleasingly simple grilles. Charger again featured hidden headlamps but was now a notchback hardtop with semi-fastback "flying buttress" roofline.

Sporty models continued to proliferate for '68. Dart added a plush GTS hardtop and convertible with standard 340 V-8 (an enlarged 273) with 275 bhp; a big 300-bhp 383 was optional. Expanding the Coronet line at mid-season was the budget-priced Super Bee, a no-frills two-door muscle coupe with a special 335-bhp 383, Dodge's counterpart to Plymouth's fantastically successful Road Runner. These and the Coronet/Charger R/Ts made up what Dodge called the "Scat Pack," identified by bumblebee stripes around the tail. All ranked among 1968's quickest and most roadable performance machines.

Along with Chrysler and Plymouth Fury, the '69 Polara/ Monaco arrived with all-new "fuselage" styling, but retained a 122-inch wheelbase. Dart, Coronet, and Charger wore minor facelifts. Bolstering the Dart line was the Swinger, a reinstated two-door hardtop that had special identifying trim, bright aluminum grille, and a choice of 318 or 340 V-8s.

Pride of the '69 fleet was the Charger Daytona, conceived for long-distance NASCAR trials like the Daytona 500 and marked by a unique bullet nose with hidden headlights and "bib" spoiler, plus a flush-window fastback roof and a huge trunklid wing on towering twin stabilizers. All this made the Daytona about 20 percent more aerodynamic than previous racing Chargers, which gave it an advantage at the Florida track of about 500 yards per lap. Dodge built only 505, just enough to qualify as a "production car" for NASCAR purposes. The strategy worked: A Daytona won the Talledega 500 in September 1969, though that was partly because the Ford contingent didn't show. In 1970, the Daytonas and Plymouth's similar Superbirds won 38 of 48 major NASCAR races. Dodge also offered a wingless, blunt-nose Charger 500 for '69 at a bit under $3900.

No doubt about it: The Sixties was a great decade for Dodge. A pity it would take two more decades before the division could build anything nearly so exciting.

DODGE AT A GLANCE, 1960-1969										
	1960	1961	1962	1963	1964	1965	1966	1967	1968	1969
Price Range, $	2278-3621	1979-3409	1951-3407	1983-3407	1988-3420	2074-3527	2094-3604	2187-3712	2323-3869	2400-4046
Weight Range, lbs.	3385-4220	2585-4125	2495-4055	2605-4186	2615-4185	2645-4355	2665-4315	2710-4475	2705-4360	2795-4361
Wheelbases, in.	118-122	106.5-122	106.5-122	106-122	106-122	106-121	106-121	111-122	111-122	111-122
6 Cyl. Engines, hp		101-145	101-145	101-145	101-145	101-145	101-145	115-145	115-145	115-145
8 Cyl. Engines, hp	230-330	230-375	230-420	230-425	180-425	180-425	180-425	180-425	190-425	190-425

A comedy of errors or a victim of bad timing? The Edsel was both—proof that what seems good today may not be tomorrow.

It was born in the heady climate of Ford Motor Company's strong, early-Fifties recovery, part of ambitious plans for a GM-like five-make hierarchy. Edsel's specific mission was to bolster Mercury—logical, as the medium-price field looked unlimited.

But with the industry's usual three-year lead time, Edsel didn't appear until late 1957, by which time the entire market was depressed. Ford had hoped to sell 100,000 for '58 but managed only a little over 63,000. Though that wasn't bad, all things considered, it was the best Edsel would do. After fewer than 45,000 for '59 and a mere 2846 of the token 1960 models, Edsel was discontinued in November 1959.

Though actually conceived as a "super Mercury," Edsel wound up a lower-medium car. The '58 line comprised no fewer than 18 models: Ford-based Rangers, Pacers, and wagons, and Mercury-based Corsairs and Citations. Distinction was achieved through gimmicky features, potent big-block V-8s, and styling that proved woefully controversial, especially the "horse collar" vertical grille. But such superficial differences weren't nearly enough in that difficult market, and disappointing sales prompted a slimmer '59 fleet of Corsairs, Rangers, and Villager wagons, all basically reskinned Fords with toned-down styling and somewhat thriftier engines.

Corsair and the largest V-8 departed for 1960, as did the vertical grille, replaced by a split horizontal affair à la '59 Pontiac (purely a coincidence). Apart from that, this last Edsel was just the all-new 1960 Ford with different trim and odd, vertical taillamps. A 292-cubic-inch V-8 of 185 horsepower was standard, with a 145-bhp 223 six a no-cost option. Another $58 bought a 300-bhp 352 "Super Express" V-8 capable of 0-60 mph in less than 10 seconds.

Models were again trimmed, this time from 10 to seven: base and deluxe Ranger two- and four-door sedans and hardtops; deluxe-trim Ranger convertible; and six- and nine-passenger Villager wagons. Options as before included two- and three-speed automatic transmissions, power steering, and air conditioning. The Ranger convertible listed at $3000, but could be optioned up to $3800.

Edsel's aborted 1960 production run makes these last models the rarest of the marque's three model years. And rare they are: only 76 ragtops, 135 hardtop sedans, 295 hardtop coupes, 777 two-door sedans, 1288 four-door sedans, and 275 Villager wagons. Among the rarest Edsel of all is the three-seat model: just 59 built.

As Detroit's biggest and most public flop since the Tucker, the Edsel reportedly lost Ford some $250 million. But this was hardly a total loss. In expanding for Edsel production, Ford was left with facilities that were applied to benefit its new 1960 Falcon, which immediately ran away with the compact market (see Ford).

Had it been a truly different car introduced three to five years either side of '58, the Edsel might be with us yet. As it is, it remains an artifact of that cynical time when Detroit thought the public couldn't tell the difference between style and substance.

1960 Ranger convertible coupe

1960 Ranger four-door sedan

1960 Villager wagon

EDSEL AT A GLANCE, 1960	
	1960
Price Range, $	2643-3072
Weight Range, lbs.	3601-4046
Wheelbases, in.	120
6 Cyl. Engines, hp	145
8 Cyl. Engines, hp	185-300

FORD

ord's history in the Sixties closely parallels that of arch-rival Chevrolet. At decade's end, Ford was also selling about 400,000 more cars per year than in 1960 after expanding into important new markets including economy compacts, intermediates, and sportier versions of regular production models. Also like Chevy, Ford built these diverse types on relatively few wheelbases. (The Mustang "ponycar" and the personal-luxury Thunderbird, the two most specialized Fords, are treated separately.)

Key management changes occurred early on. Lee A. Iacocca took charge as Ford Division general manager in 1960, while Eugene Bordinat became Dearborn design chief on the departure of George Walker the following year. Iacocca soon put an end to the mundane people-movers favored by his predecessor, Robert S. McNamara. By 1970, Ford was offering some of the world's best road cars. In fact, Fords were the cars to beat on the nation's race tracks and dragstrips for much of the decade. Dodge's 1969 Charger, for example, was an all-out effort to halt the Ford superstockers.

The division also evolved from Chevy-follower to Chevy-leader in the Sixties. Ford's compact Falcon outsold the Corvair, its 1962 mid-size Fairlane was two years ahead of Chevelle, and its phenomenally successful Mustang sent Chevrolet racing to the drawing boards to develop the Camaro.

The best way to summarize Fords of the Sixties is by size. The smallest was Falcon, which rode a 109.5-inch wheelbase through 1965, then a 110.9-inch span (113 for wagons). Two- and four-door sedans and four-door wagons were always offered, while convertibles and hardtop coupes were added for 1963-65, all with unit construction.

For some, the early Falcon was the ultimate "throwaway" car: built to sell at a low price and designed to be discarded within five years (some said one year). To others, though, it was the reincarnation of the Model A: cheap but cheerful, simple but not unacceptably spartan. Falcon's conventional suspension and cast-iron six (mostly a 170-cubic-inch unit of 101 horsepower) certainly looked dull next to Corvair engineering, but they made for friendly, roomy little cars that rode well and delivered 20-25 mpg. Falcons were also easily serviced by "shadetree mechanics," something that could definitely *not* be said for the complicated compact Chevy. Though Falcon sales gradually declined as the decade wore on, largely due to competition from both inside and outside Ford Division, the line was always profitable.

Replying to Chevy's hot-selling Corvair Monza in the spring of 1961 was the bucket-seat Futura two-door, which along with other Falcons was reskinned for 1964-65 with less distinctive, squared-off lines. The prime collector Falcon is the mid-1963 Futura Sprint, a pretty convertible and hardtop coupe available with the lively new small-block Fairlane V-8, initially a 260 with 164 bhp, then a 289 with about 200 bhp for '65. It was one fine engine, which helps explain why its later 302-cid V-8 survived into the Nineties. It completely transformed Falcon performance without greatly affecting mileage. Sprints offered special trim, bucket seats, console, and full instrumentation including a 6000-rpm tachometer. When equipped with the optional four-speed manual transmission, they were great fun to drive.

1960 Galaxie Victoria hardtop sedan

1960 Galaxie Starliner hardtop coupe

1960 Falcon two-door sedan

1961 Galaxie Sunliner convertible coupe

The 1966 Falcons were basically shortened versions of that year's new Fairlane, with the same sort of curvy, GM-inspired styling and long-hood/short-deck proportions *à la* Mustang. Falcon would continue in this form through early 1970. In its last year before emission controls, the 289 packed 225 bhp in "Stage 2" tune with four-barrel carburetor, and made for some very fast Falcons. For 1968 it was detuned to 195 bhp, but its 302 enlargement arrived as an option. With two-barrel carb, the 302 ran on regular gas and delivered 210 bhp. With four barrel, it delivered 230 bhp on premium fuel, though emission controls soon put an end to that version. Falcon's lineal successor was the Maverick, announced in early '69 for 1970.

Ford broke new ground for 1962 with the mid-size Fairlane, basically a bigger Falcon on a 115.5-inch wheelbase. Its concept was much like that of Virgil Exner's downsized '62 Plymouths and Dodges. But unlike Chrysler, Ford retained its full-size Customs and Galaxies—a wise move, even though Fairlane sold more than 297,000 units its first year and over 300,000 for '63.

The Fairlane was significant for introducing Ford's brilliant small-block V-8, the basis for some of its most memorable Sixties cars. Bored out to 289 cid as a '63 Fairlane option, it delivered up to 271 bhp—almost one horsepower per cubic inch. Powerful and smooth, yet surprisingly economical, it was the definitive small V-8. Tuned versions in sports-racers like the Shelby Cobra and mid-engine Ford GT40 disproved the old saying about there being no substitute for cubic inches. In fact, the GT40 nearly took the world GT Manufacturers Championship away from Ferrari in 1964, its first full season. (With big-block power, Ford GTs went on to win the Le Mans 24-Hours, the world's most prestigious sports-car endurance race, two years in a row, 1966-67.)

Initially, Fairlane offered two- and four-door sedans in base and sportier 500 trim, plus a pillared 500 Sport Coupe with standard bucket seats. Four-door wagons and a brace of hardtop coupes arrived for '63. Beginning with the '64s, Ford offered a growing assortment of handling and performance options.

Fairlane was completely rebodied for '66 on a 116-inch wheelbase (113 for wagons), gaining a sleek, tailored look highlighted by curved side glass, stacked quad headlamps, and tidy vertical taillights. Heading that year's line was the bucket-seat 500XL hardtop coupe and convertible in base and GT trim. Standard XLs came with a 120-bhp 200-cid six, but most were ordered with optional 289 V-8s. GTs carried a standard 390 big-block with a potent 335 bhp. This engine could be ordered on any Fairlane, and racers were quick to put it in the lighter two-door sedans, which earned respect for their competitive prowess.

With no change in wheelbases, another body and styling change occurred for 1968, when Fairlane and Fairlane 500 models were joined by a new Torino series as Ford's plushest mid-sizers. A 115-bhp 200 six was standard for all but the Torino GT convertible, hardtop coupe, and new fastback hardtop (all duplicated in the 500 line), which came with the 210-bhp 302 V-8 as well as buckets-and-console interior, pinstriping, and more performance options than a salesman could memorize.

1962 Galaxie 500 Victoria hardtop coupe

1962 Galaxie 500 XL Sunliner convertible coupe

1962 Falcon Futura Sports Coupe

1963 Fairlane 500 hardtop coupe

1963 Galaxie 500 XL hardtop coupe

1963 Galaxie 500 XL convertible coupe

The '69s were largely unchanged, but new fastback and notchback Torino Cobra hardtops arrived, the name borrowed from Carroll Shelby's muscular Ford-powered sports cars. These packed the 335-bhp 428 V-8 that had first appeared in the "1968½" Mercury Cyclone as the "Cobra Jet." A $133 option was "Ram-Air," a fiberglass hood scoop with special air cleaner assembly that ducted incoming air directly to the carburetor (via a valve in the air cleaner). Four-speed gearbox, stiff suspension, and competition-style hood tie-downs were standard. One magazine was actually disappointed when its Cobra ran 0-60 mph in "only" 7.2 seconds and the standing quarter-mile in 15 sec-

onds at 98.3 miles per hour. On the other hand, just about everyone admitted that of all the '69 "supercars"—Plymouth GTX, Dodge Charger R/T, Pontiac GTO, Chevelle 396, and Buick GS400—the Torino Cobra was the tightest, the best built, and the quietest.

These Torinos were potent racing machines. Ford discovered that the styling of the counterpart Mercury Cyclone was slightly more aerodynamic, and thus usually entered them in stock-car contests over 250 miles long. Nevertheless, a race-prepped Torino or Cyclone could achieve about 190 mph. Lee Roy Yarborough won the '69 Daytona 500 in a Ford.

1963 Galaxie 500 hardtop coupe

1963 Falcon Futura Sprint hardtop coupe

1964 Galaxie 500 XL convertible coupe

1964 Falcon Futura Sprint convertible coupe

With the advent of the Thunderbird and then the Falcon, the Custom, pre-1962 Fairlane, and Galaxie models became the "standard" or full-sized Fords. For 1960 these cars swelled to a 119-inch wheelbase that they would keep through 1968, after which it was stretched two inches. Most big Fords of this decade were heavy and not rewarding to drive on anything but a superhighway, though certain variations of these 3000- to 4000-pound cruisers were surprisingly capable on winding roads.

The big 1960 Fords gained an all-new body that would persist through four facelifts: two minor, two major. The '60s were much longer, lower, wider, and sleeker than the boxy '59s, and even mimicked Chevy's bat-fins a little, but looked good with their chrome-edged fender lines and bigger new glass areas. The Skyliner was gone, but a sleek semi-fastback Starliner hardtop coupe replaced it in the Galaxie series. Though less popular than the square-roof styles, its shape was just the thing for NASCAR racing.

Starliner bowed out after 1961, when standard styling was facelifted via a full-width '59-style concave grille and a return to round taillights, capped by discreet blades. That year's top engine option was the new 390-cid version of the 1958-vintage FE-series big-block, offering 300 bhp or, on a very limited basis, 375 and 401 bhp in high-tune "Interceptor" form.

A chunkier, more "important" look marked the '62 standards, grouped into Galaxie (replacing the previous Custom 300) and new Galaxie 500 series, with roughly the same model choices as before. Reflecting the buckets-and-console craze then sweeping Detroit were the mid-season 500XL Victoria hardtop coupe and Sunliner convertible. The "500" stood for the 500-mile NASCAR races the division was winning. (Ford won every 500 in '63.) "XL" purportedly meant "Xtra Lively." Though the standard powertrain was a 170-bhp 292 V-8 with Cruise-O-Matic, options could turn the big XL into a real fire-breather. There were 300-, 340-, and 375-bhp 390s and a new bored-out 406-cid V-8 with 385 and 405 bhp, plus Borg-Warner four-speed gearbox. An even bigger bore for '63 produced a 427-cid powerhouse with 410/425 bhp. High prices—around $400—made these engines uncommon.

New lower-body sheetmetal gave the '63 "Super-Torque" Galaxies a cleaner, leaner look, announced by a simple concave grille. A pair of cheap "300" sedans returned (renamed Custom/Custom 500 for '64), and there was some mid-year excitement in the form of 500 and 500XL Sports two-door hardtops with thin-pillar "slantback" rooflines. Though a bit starchier-looking than the old Starliner, these, too, were aimed right at the stock-car ovals.

The final and most substantial restyle on the big 1960 body occurred for '64, bringing heavily sculptured lower-body sheetmetal, a complex grille, and slantback rooflines for all closed models. The entire Ford line won *Motor Trend* magazine's "Car of the Year" award, partly because of the division's ever-widening "Total Performance" advertising and competition campaign. Performance was just what these big Fords had, with available small-block and big-block V-8s offering from 195 up to a rousing 425 bhp. With a 390, an XL could scale 0-60 mph in 9.3 seconds; the 427 reduced that to 7.4 seconds. The one major complaint was

1965 Galaxie 500 XL hardtop coupe

1966 Galaxie 500 7-Litre hardtop coupe

1966 Fairlane 500 XL GT convertible coupe

1967 Fairlane 500 XL hardtop coupe

1967 Galaxie 500 XL convertible coupe

the cars' marked tendency to nosedive in "panic" stops, aggravated by slightly touchy power brakes.

Ford had its best NASCAR year ever in 1965, its big cars running for the last time but winning 48 of the 55 scheduled events. Luxury, however, got most of the showroom emphasis that year. All-new except for engines, the '65s were distinguished by simpler, more linear styling announced by stacked quad headlamps. Underneath was a stronger chassis with a completely new front suspension. Arriving at mid-year were the Galaxie 500 LTD hardtop coupe and sedan, the poshest big Fords yet. The priciest, too, at about $3300. Ads proclaimed LTD as quiet as a Rolls-Royce at speed. Times were changing. With intermediates taking over in competition, the big Fords no longer needed a performance image as sales support.

The '65 standards got a minor touchup for '66, and LTDs gained new "7-Litre" companions, powered by the Thun-derbird's big new 345-bhp 428 engine. The following year brought new outer sheetmetal with more flowing contours and "faster" rooflines on hardtop coupes. LTD became a separate three-model series, adding a four-door sedan but losing the 7-Litre sub-models. Hidden-headlamp grilles marked the '68 LTDs and Galaxie XLs.

A new bodyshell arrived for '69 with a two-inch longer wheelbase, "tunneled" backlight for newly named "SportsRoof" fastback models, and ventless door glass on hardtops and convertibles. LTD continued to find increasing favor. Ford had built nearly 139,000 in '68; the '69s saw more than twice that many.

Ford kept pace with Chevrolet in the Sixties production race and actually beat it for model years 1961 and '66. Helped greatly by the Mustang, the company recorded its first two-million-car year in 1965—proof positive that Ford often did have some "better ideas."

1968 Torino GT convertible coupe

1969 Torino Cobra hardtop coupe

1969 Torino GT fastback hardtop coupe

1969 Torino Talladega Sport Roof hardtop coupe

FORD AT A GLANCE, 1960-1969										
	1960	1961	1962	1963	1964	1965	1966	1967	1968	1969
Price Range, $	1912-2967	1914-3013	1985-3518	1985-3088	1996-3498	2020-3872	2060-3493	2118-3493	2252-3619	2283-3738
Weight Range, lbs.	2259-4072	2254-4015	2243-4022	2300-4003	2365-3998	2366-3937	2519-4059	2520-4030	2680-4059	2700-4227
Wheelbases, in.	109.5-119	109.5-119	109.5-119	109.5-119	109.5-119	109.5-119	111-119	111-119	111-119	111-121
6 Cyl. Engines, hp	90-145	85-135	85-138	85-138	85-138	101-150	105-150	105-150	100-150	100-155
8 Cyl. Engines, hp	185-360	175-401	145-405	145-425	164-425	200-425	200-425	200-425	195-390	220-360

Mustang, the original "ponycar," was Detroit's greatest single success of the Sixties. It not only lifted Ford's 1965 model-year volume by well over a half-million units, but set an all-time record for first-year new-model sales. A total of 680,989 were sold between the April 1964 introduction and August 1965 (when production switched to '66 models). Truck drivers drove through showroom windows while staring at them, housewives entered contests to win them, and dealers auctioned them off amidst initial demand that exceeded supply by 15-to-1. America loved the Mustang.

Spearheading this remarkable achievement was Lee A. Iacocca, the car salesman who had worked his way from an obscure position in Pennsylvania to become Ford Division general manager in 1960. The idea was simplicity itself: a low-cost "personal car." People had been pleading with Ford to revive the two-seat Thunderbird since its demise in 1957. Four years later, Iacocca and company began planning a new young-person's car that would be inexpensive to build, peppy, sporty-looking, and priced to sell for less than $2500. Projected annual volume was 100,000 units, which, of course, proved to be far too conservative.

The very first Mustang was a low, two-seat fiberglass roadster with a 90-inch wheelbase and a mid-mounted 2.0-liter V-4 developing 90 horsepower. Strictly an experimental, it was pretty but impractical. As Iacocca said, "That's sure not the car we want to build, because it can't be a volume car. It's too far out." But dozens of prototypes followed, culminating in the conventional, four-seat 108-inch-wheelbase production Mustang of "1964½." From a marketing standpoint, it was perfect.

1965 Mustang fastback coupe

Throughout the Sixties, Mustang was offered as a hardtop coupe, convertible, and fastback coupe. The crisp notchback hardtop would always be the sales leader by far. Convertible orders started at the 100,000 level, but fell to less than 15,000 a year by 1969. The fastback, initially a seminotch style called "2+2," arrived in autumn 1964 with the rest of the '65 Ford line. It soon overtook the convertible in sales, averaging about 50,000 a year through 1970.

Standard power for the first six months of production came from the 170-cubic-inch Falcon six (101 bhp) and 260-cid V-8 (164 bhp). A 200-cid six (120 bhp) and the bored-out 289 small-block V-8 (200-271 bhp) then took over. Increasingly hairy big-block options were offered before government regulations put an end to Ford's "Total Performance" program: for 1967, a 320-bhp 390; for 1968, a 427 with 390 bhp; for 1969, a 335-bhp 428.

Much of Mustang's appeal stemmed from numerous op-

1964½ Mustang convertible coupe

1965 Mustang fastback coupe

tions that enabled customers to personalize the car. Careful use of the order form could produce a cute economy job, thundering drag racer, deceptively nimble sporty car, or a compact luxury-liner. Transmission choices comprised automatics, three- and four-speed manuals, and stick-overdrive. Handling packages, power steering, disc brakes, air conditioning, and tachometer were always available, as was a bench front seat to substitute for the standard buckets, though few people ordered it. A GT package option delivered a pleasant assortment of goodies including front-disc brakes, full instrumentation, and special badges. Also available were a variety of interior trims, along with accent stripes and special moldings for the exterior.

Mustang styling was inspirational, the work of Joe Oros,

1965 Mustang convertible coupe

1966 Mustang convertible coupe

1967 Mustang GTA hardtop coupe

1968 Mustang fastback coupe

1969 Mustang Mach 1 fastback coupe

L. David Ash, and Gail Halderman of the Ford Division studio. Its long-hood/short-deck proportions quickly became Detroit *de rigeur*, particularly for the imitators that soon became known, in Mustang's honor, as "ponycars." The basic '65 design saw careful refinement in the first four years, with '66s changed only in detail. A deeper grille, revised taillamps, and sculptured side panels ending in twin simulated air scoops marked the '67s, along with a full-fastback roof for the 2+2. The '68s were identified by a revised grille with recessed galloping-horse emblem, plus federally required side marker lights and minor trim changes.

This relative sameness plus increasing competition after 1966 and a steady decline in ponycar demand from about 1967 all took a toll in Mustang sales. After an impressive 607,500 units for '66, volume dropped to 472,000, then to 317,000 for '68.

The package was more extensively revised for 1969: lower, longer, wider, and more exaggerated, with ventless side glass, quad headlamps, and a more imposing dash. A new Mach 1 fastback with firm suspension and a standard 250-bhp 351 V-8 joined the line at $3139. It stood apart from the standard "SportsRoof" via a special grille with driving lamps, matte-black center hood section with functional air scoop, quick-fill gas cap, and black honeycomb rear appliqué. Catering to the luxury market was the new Grande notchback, priced at $2866/$2971 with standard six/V-8 and offering landau-style black or white vinyl roof, racing-type mirrors, special i.d. script, and bright wheel-well moldings.

Making an even bigger splash for mid-1969 was the fastback Boss 302, a $3588 roadgoing version of the Mustangs then cleaning up in the Trans-American racing series.

Though its 302 small-block delivered an alleged 290 bhp, estimates pegged output at closer to 400. Only 1934 were built for the model year, another 6318 for 1970. All had special striping, front "chin" spoiler, Mach 1-style rear wing, and distinctive rear-window louvers.

A horse of a different color was the big-block Boss 429. Tagged at $4798, it was stuffed full of Ford's Cobra Jet NASCAR engine with cast-magnesium head covers and semi-hemispherical combustion chambers. Just 858 were built for '69 and another 498 to 1970 specifications. All were largely custom-crafted, as considerable front metalwork was required to accommodate the bulky 429.

Mustang is still with us, of course, and better than ever in many ways. But the 1965-66 originals are the most highly collectible of the breed, though the 1967-68s are coming on strong. All offer sports-car fun, room for four, and good looks at prices that remain reasonable even on the collector market and can only go higher. No wonder America still loves these Mustangs.

MUSTANG AT A GLANCE, 1965-1969					
	1965	**1966**	**1967**	**1968**	**1969**
Price Range, $	2372-2614	2416-2653	2461-2698	2602-2814	2635-4798
Weight Range, lbs.	2583-2789	2488-2650	2568-2738	2635-2745	2798-3210
Wheelbases, in.	108	108	108	108	108
6 Cyl. Engines, hp	101-120	120	120	115-155	115-155
8 Cyl. Engines, hp	164-271	200-271	200-320	195-390	220-375

Ford's decision to abandon its jaunty, two-seat "personal car" for a larger, four-seat Thunderbird was brilliant. Since nicknamed "Squarebird" by its many admirers, the square-cut 1958-60 generation stands as America's first high-volume "personal-luxury" car, pioneering the sporty buckets-and-console interior that most all Detroit would be obliged to imitate in the Sixties. Equally influential was the Squarebird hardtop's formal wide-quarter roofline. Destined to be a T-Bird hallmark for the next 20-plus years, it boosted sales when applied to other closed Fords in the Sixties, and would also be mimicked by rival companies.

Speaking of sales, the Squarebird greatly exceeded all expectations, making a hero of its chief backer, Ford Division general manager Robert S. McNamara. By 1960, annual T-Bird sales were almost five times as high as in 1957, the best two-seater year.

Though not vastly different from the 1958-59 models, the final Squarebird of 1960 was somewhat more glittery, sporting a complex grille with a prominent horizontal bar bisecting three vertical bars on a mesh background, plus new triple rear lamp clusters and small trim changes. Engines and basic design were unchanged: a unitized, 113-inch-wheelbase convertible and hardtop coupe with standard 352-cubic-inch, 300-horsepower V-8 driving through three-speed Cruise-O-Matic self-shift transmission. As before, a Lincoln 430 V-8 with 350 bhp was optional. Prices averaged about $4000. Returning to U.S. production for the first time since before World War II was a slide-back metal sunroof, a new hardtop option that year. Volume continued climbing, reaching near 91,000 units, a figure T-Bird would not exceed until 1964. Hardtops outsold convertibles nearly 8-to-1, showing that Bird buyers wanted luxury first and sportiness second.

A new third-generation Bird arrived for 1961, and would see only detail changes through 1963. Distinctive styling was highlighted by pointy front fenders, small "blade" fins above big circular taillamps, and bulging bodysides bereft of sheetmetal sculpturing (except on the '63s, when a modest half-length creaseline appeared above each front wheel-arch). There was now just one engine: a 352 stroked to 390 cid, though rated horsepower was unchanged. An extra-cost M-series version with three two-barrel carburetors instead of a single four-barrel delivered 40 bhp more for 1962-63. With minor alterations, the 390 would remain Thunderbird's basic powerplant through 1968, accompanied by even bigger big-block options beginning in '66.

Third-generation engineering was conservative but sound. Ford had considered front-wheel drive, but felt it too unorthodox for this market. Instead, engineers stressed quality control, solid construction, high ride comfort, and minimum noise at speed. Extensive use of rubber bushings for the coil-spring independent front and leaf-spring rear suspensions made these Thunderbirds among the best-riding cars of the day.

Two interesting derivatives were added for '62: the Sports Roadster and the Landau. (The former was the only production four-seat car to become a two-seater.) Newly installed Ford Division chief Lee A. Iacocca okayed it because dealers had been besieged with requests for a car like the 1955-57 Bird. He decided there was no significant market for anything like that, but a semi-sports model wouldn't hurt.

The designer most responsible for the Sports Roadster was Bud Kaufman, who developed a fiberglass tonneau for concealing the rear seat, thus turning the normal convertible into a "two-seater." Twin front-seat headrests were formed into the tonneau's leading edge, and sloped down

1960 Thunderbird hardtop coupe

1961 Thunderbird convertible coupe

1962 Thunderbird Sports Roadster convertible coupe

1963 Thunderbird hardtop coupe

sharply to the rear before fading away near the aft edge. Kaufman overcame fitting problems so that the soft top could be operated with the tonneau in place. Completing the package were Kelsey-Hayes chrome wire wheels with knock-off hubs that dictated omitting the stock rear fender skirts (due to insufficient clearance).

Stunning though it was, the Sports Roadster didn't sell. The problem was price: about $650 more than the standard convertible, a hefty $5439 in all. As a result, only 1427 of the '62s found buyers and just 455 of the '63s, after which the Sports Roadster disappeared. Ford dealers sold a similar tonneau and wire wheels as accessories for the '64 convertible, but these are even scarcer today.

The Landau was more popular by far. For $4398, only $77 more than the standard hardtop, you got a vinyl-covered roof with a fake S-shape "landau" bar on each rear pillar, plus a somewhat spiffier cabin. Those extras may not sound like much, but buyers flocked to the Landau. By 1966 it was outselling the unadorned hardtop, and would generate the bulk of T-Bird sales three years later. Extending the idea for 1963 was a Limited Edition Landau, introduced for the spring selling season. True to its name, it saw only 2000 copies, all with a special numbered console plaque, all-white vinyl interior, and spinner wheel covers.

Though Thunderbird production was down in these years, it remained far higher than in the two-seater days. The respective totals for model years 1961-63 were 73,000, 78,000, and about 63,300.

Following its usual three-year design cycle and with wheelbase again unchanged, Thunderbird was completely revamped for 1964, bearing all-new sheetmetal that now included busy bodyside sculpturing. This generation would carry on without major change through '66, though quiet, refined luxury received increasing emphasis as convertible sales declined noticeably. The open Thunderbird was thus consigned to history after 1966, when it accounted for only 7.5 percent of total series production. T-Bird output reached a new high of close to 92,500 for '64, then eased to around 75,000 for '65, followed by just over 69,000 in '66.

Among features introduced with the fourth generation were a cockpit-style passenger compartment and "Silent-Flo" ventilation; full-width taillight housings, including backup lights and sequential turn signals; standard front-disc brakes (1965); and a formal "Town" roofline sans rear side windows for the Landau and hardtop (1966). A popular accessory offered since 1961 was the "Swing-Away" steering wheel. With the transmission in "Park," it could be shifted laterally about ten inches inboard to facilitiate driver entry/exit. The 300-bhp 390 remained the only engine through 1965, after which it gained 15 horsepower. For 1966, a 428 big-block rated at 345 bhp arrived as an optional alternative; it would continue through '67.

Ford officials debated the pros and cons of a Thunderbird sedan throughout the Sixties. Furthermore, by mid-decade, Iacocca was convinced that enthusiast buyers were being satisfied by other Fords—namely the Mustang "ponycar" and an attractive array of Falcons and Fairlanes. Market surveys showed that the Thunderbird, firmly entrenched in the personal-luxury market it helped create, no longer required anything resembling a "performance image."

1963 Thunderbird Sports Roadster convertible coupe

1963 Thunderbird convertible coupe

1964 Thunderbird convertible coupe

1965 Thunderbird convertible coupe

1965 Thunderbird Limited Edition Special Landau hardtop coupe

1966 Thunderbird Town Landau hardtop coupe

1967 Thunderbird Landau four-door sedan

1968 Thunderbird Landau four-door sedan

Reflecting this conclusion was a completely restyled group of 1967 models that included a new four-door Landau on a 117.2-inch wheelbase. The hardtop and two-door Landau returned on a new 114.7-inch span. Front ends displayed a deeply recessed honeycomb grille with concealed headlamps and a bumper wrapped underneath. Rear quarter windows on two-doors retracted horizontally into the roof pillars. Engines were unchanged.

The fifth-generation Bird would continue through 1971 despite sales that trended mostly downward. The Landau sedan wasn't very practical—especially its rear-hinged back doors, a Thirties throwback—declining from almost 25,000 first-year sales to slightly more than 8400 by 1970. Volume as a whole sank from 78,000 to a little more than 49,000 for '69, then recovered to just above the 50,000 mark.

Styling changes were minor through decade's end. The '68s bore narrowed rocker moldings and an eggcrate grille pattern replaced the '67 honeycomb. For '69, horizontal louvers and three vertical dividers made up the grille, divided taillamps replaced the full-width ensemble, and rear quarter windows were eliminated on the Landau coupe.

Absent since '61, the electric sliding sunroof returned as an option for any vinyl-roof model.

Newly enacted federal standards affected Thunderbird as much as any American car at decade's end. Side marker lights, energy-absorbing steering column, seatbelts, non-impacting interior surfaces, and other safety measures were mandated for '68. Limits on tailpipe emissions were satisfied for '69 by switching to a new big-block 429 V-8 as the one and only available engine. Though rated at 360 bhp, 15 bhp more than the superseded 428, the 429 was designed not for top-end power but low-revving torque and durability. It was also more amenable to being tuned for minimum emissions without compromising drivability. The veteran 390, which had powered T-Birds for eight years, was simultaneously dropped, though it would continue for a time in other Fords.

Still with us after all these years, few current models can boast of a longer lifespan than the Thunderbird. Though its mission may have changed from time to time, it has always been one of the highlights of Ford's passenger car line—and probably always will be.

THUNDERBIRD AT A GLANCE, 1960-1969										
	1960	1961	1962	1963	1964	1965	1966	1967	1968	1969
Price Range, $	3755-4222	4170-4637	4321-5439	4445-5563	4486-4953	4486-4953	4426-4879	4603-4825	4716-4924	4824-5043
Weight Range, lbs.	3799-3897	3958-4130	4132-4471	4195-4396	4431-4586	4470-4588	4359-4496	4248-4348	4366-4458	4348-4460
Wheelbases, in.	113	113	113	113	113	113	113	115-117	115-117	115-117
8 Cyl. Engines, hp	300-350	300	300-340	300-340	300	300	315-345	315-345	315-360	360

IMPERIAL

I mperial became a distinct make for 1955 and remained so for two consecutive decades. Since the late Twenties, the name had been reserved for the most luxurious Chryslers—and that would prove a problem. Somehow, Imperial would never escape its Chrysler heritage, which would limit its success in the prestige-conscious luxury field as much as anything.

As cars, Imperial's best years as a separate make were its first two. In sales, its best year was 1957, which brought the first of the heroically finned models shaped by Chrysler design chief Virgil M. Exner. After this, Imperial was strictly an also-ran. Cadillac continued as the overwhelming luxury leader, with Lincoln a distant second, and Imperial an even more distant third.

Though late-Fifties and early-Sixties Imperials bring grimaces from designers now, they seemed perfectly valid at the time. The 1960 models were built on Chrysler's largest standard wheelbase (129 inches); a 149.5-inch stretch continued for custom-built Crown Imperial limousines. Unlike other 1960 Chrysler products, which adopted "unibody construction," Imperial retained body-on-frame, which was more readily amenable in those days to noise and road shock isolation, necessary for the level of smoothness and silence luxury buyers demanded. Also carrying on from 1957-59 was Chrysler's torsion-bar front suspension, which made Imperials a tad more nimble than luxury rivals, though they were still quite ponderous. The powertrain, as in '59, comprised a 413-cubic-inch wedgehead V-8 producing 350 bhp on 10:1 compression and premium fuel, mated to Chrysler's excellent three-speed TorqueFlite automatic transmission, new for '57.

Imperial's 1960 lineup was also a '59 repeat: Custom, mid-range Crown, and top-shelf LeBaron series in ascending order, each separated by about $600. All offered a four-door sedan and Southampton hardtop sedan. Southampton hardtop coupes were limited to Custom and Crown, and the latter offered Imperial's only convertible, a slow seller at $5774; only 618 were built for the model year. Overall production was about the same as in 1959: some 17,700, a far cry from the near 38,000 of best-ever '57.

Though evolved from basic 1957-59 appearance, Imperial styling became cartoonish for 1960, marked by swollen tailfins, a florid grille, and an even larger windshield. Interiors were ornate, dominated by an impressively bright, complicated dash with a plethora of pushbuttons, and an odd, squarish steering wheel. Comfort was emphasized with a new high-back driver's seat padded in thick foam rubber, adjustable "spot" air conditioning, six-way power seat with a single rotary control, Auto-Pilot cruise control, and automatic headlamp dimmer. Customs were upholstered in pretty crown-pattern nylon; Crowns in wool, leather, or nylon and vinyl; LeBarons in wool broadcloth.

The long-wheelbase Crown limousines built by Italy's Ghia coachworks in 1957-65 generally followed each year's Imperial styling. Ghia was tapped for this assignment because Chrysler could not economically build such customs in Detroit. Against projected domestic tooling costs of $3.3 million, Ghia could build Crown Imperials for only $15,000 apiece, though Chrysler helped by shipping "starter kits" to the Ghia factory in Turin.

Each Ghia limousine began as an unfinished two-door hardtop on a rigid convertible chassis, albeit with all body panels intact. Ghia cut the car apart, added 20.5 inches to the wheelbase, reworked the superstructure, fitted and trimmed the luxurious interior, and finished off the bodies with 150 pounds of lead filler. Each car required a month

1960 Custom four-door sedan

1961 LeBaron Southampton hardtop sedan

1962 LeBaron Southampton hardtop sedan

1963 Custom Southampton hardtop sedan

1963 Custom Southampton hardtop sedan

to complete, and production during the Sixties never came to more than 16 in any model year. All were impeccably tailored ultra-luxury conveyances.

The new 1960 bodyshell was considerably changed for 1961—and hardly for the better. Fins were the most blatant ever to appear on an Imperial: high and gull-like, carrying Imperial's trademark "gunsight" taillamps. And there was a new gimmick: freestanding headlamps, individual chrome bullets on tiny pedestals nestled within severely pocketed front fenders—another of Exner's "classic" throwbacks. This strange idea would persist through 1963, but rear styling became much more tasteful. Four-door pillared sedans were eliminated for '61, but other offerings returned along with the previous powerteam. "Sci-fi" styling, Chrysler's now-widespread reputation for indifferent workmanship, and a handsome, more compact new Lincoln Continental all conspired to dampen demand. Imperial's '61 production fell to around 12,250 units.

Exner left Chrysler during 1961, but not before fashioning a truncated new Imperial as part of a downsized corporate line for 1962. It never reached production, however, which was fortunate—his shrunken Dodges and Plymouths did, and they fared poorly. Instead, the '61 was reissued with its ugly fins planed off, leaving straight-top rear fenders capped by cigar-like freestanding taillights. The 413 lost 10 bhp to detuning, but would continue in this form through 1965. Though production rose to a bit over 14,250, Imperial volume was still only about 50 percent of Lincoln's.

Another facelift gave the '63s a new grille insert made up of elongated rectangles, plus a crisper rear roofline and restyled rear deck. The stylist responsible for much of this revision was Elwood Engel, who'd come over from Ford—where he designed the aforementioned Continental—to replace Exner in mid-1961. The lineup was again unchanged, and production was about the same as for '62.

Clean, all-new Engel styling completely replaced the old Exner silhouette for 1964, Imperial becoming much like his square-lined Continental. Fenderlines were edged in brightwork, a divided grille appeared (recalling 1955), and the freestanding headlamps were replaced by integral units within the grille. One Exner touch remained, however: the simulated trunklid spare tire, though it too was now squarish, and carried down into the bumper *à la* the 1956-57 Continental Mark II. Inside, a less contrived instrument panel with strong horizontal format was a welcome change. Modelwise, the slow-selling Custom was eliminated along with the Southampton name for pillarless styles, leaving just four offerings (excluding the Ghia Crown). Sales were exceedingly good at over 23,000 units for the model year, a level that would not be approached again until 1969.

Good sales and the big '64 redesign dictated a stand-pat 1965. The only significant change was a revised grille with glass-covered headlights, plus prices bumped $100-$200 higher. Displayed at that year's New York Automobile Show was the exotic LeBaron D'Or, a customized hardtop. "D'Or" referred to gold striping and embellishments, as well as special Royal Essence Laure¹ Gold paint.

Ghia stopped building Crown limousines in 1965, but ten more were constructed in Spain using '66 grilles and

1964 Crown Imperial limousine

1965 LeBaron hardtop sedan

1966 Crown Coupe

rear decks. When Imperial finally went to unit construction for '67, Chrysler worked out a limousine program with Stageway Coaches of Fort Smith, Arkansas. Built through 1971 at the rate of about six per year, these cars, simply called LeBarons, were much larger, riding an unbelievable 163-inch wheelbase—by far the longest in the American industry. Prices ranged from $12,000 to $15,000, depending on equipment.

Once more, the Engel-styled Crowns and LeBarons returned for 1966 with only detail changes. The grille was now an eggcrate affair, with each crate holding tiny elongated rectangles, but the rear deck persisted in suggesting a fake spare. A bore increase brought the wedge-head to 440 cid, and horsepower returned to 350. Model-year production went the other way, dropping from 1965's 18,500—itself a considerable decline from '64—to fewer than 13,750.

The '67 Imperials were completely redesigned. Chrysler engineers were by now sufficiently experienced with unit construction to use it for their most expensive product, and newer technology allowed computerized stress testing of a given shape before it was built. Unibody construction also promised weight savings. And indeed, the '67s were about 100 pounds lighter than comparable '66s.

But the real reason for this switch was lackluster sales, which made a completely separate Imperial platform just

too costly to sustain. Therefore, just as it had prior to 1960, Imperial again shared basic architecture with Chrysler in the interest of reduced production costs.

Still, this was not readily apparent. Up front, the '67s displayed a high grille with a prominent nameplate and squarish fenders containing the parking lights. The rear bumper was a broad U below a full-width taillamp panel holding a large Imperial eagle medallion in a central circle. The sides were still flat, but relieved a little by "character line" moldings. Wheelbase contracted to 127 inches, the four-door pillared sedan returned without a series name, and other models continued as before. Sales moved up to 17,620, still far adrift of Lincoln's, let alone Cadillac's.

Volume dropped below 15,400 the following year and prompted a far-reaching decision: From 1969, Imperial would share Chrysler sheetmetal as well as inner structure. A casualty of this decision was the Crown convertible, which made its last appearance for '68. All models were only slightly altered from '67. Style changes included a new grille wrapped around the fenders to enclose parking and cornering lights, rear side marker lights as required by Washington, and narrow paint stripes along the beltline. Newly optional dual exhausts and twin-snorkel air cleaner coaxed 360 bhp from the 440 V-8, but it was only offered this one year.

The Chrysler-like 1969 models were among the tidiest

1967 Crown hardtop sedan

1969 LeBaron hardtop sedan

1969 LeBaron hardtop coupe

Imperials ever, their long, low-roof "fuselage styling" announced by a full-width eggcrate grille with concealed headlamps. Ventless side glass was featured on air-conditioned coupes. Overall length stretched by five inches with no change in wheelbase, yet curb weights ran about 100 pounds less. Model choices were down to hardtop coupe and sedan in Crown and LeBaron trim, plus a pillared Crown sedan priced identically with the Crown hardtop. LeBaron was no longer the $7000 semi-custom it had been, its list price being slashed by about $800 to the $5900-$6100 level. Despite fewer models, LeBaron exceed the

Crown in sales for the first time. The overall '69 total was 22,183 units, the third best in Imperial history.

Alas, an increasing resemblance to Chrysler would cause sales to drop fast in the early Seventies, leading to Imperial's demise after 1975. But it would return, first as a 1981-83 luxury coupe that didn't impress many buyers (fewer than 11,000), then for 1989 as the top-shelf version of Chrysler's newest front-drive car, the largish Y-body New Yorker. So Imperial is again very much what it was in most years before 1955—"just a Chrysler." A pity it has so often failed in trying to be more.

IMPERIAL AT A GLANCE, 1960-1969										
	1960	1961	1962	1963	1964	1965	1966	1967	1968	1969
Price Range, $	4923-16,500	4923-16,500	4920-6422	5058-18,500	5581-18,500	5772-18,500	5733-18,500	5374-15,000	5654-15,000	5592-16,000
Weight Range, lbs.	4655-5960	4715-5960	4540-4765	4640-6100	4950-6100	5015-6100	4990-6100	4780-6300	4660-6300	4555-6300
Wheelbases, in.	129-149.5	129-149.5	129	129-149.5	129-149.5	129-149.5	129-149.5	127-163	127-163	127-163
8 Cyl. Engines, hp	350	350	340	340	340	340	350	350	350-360	350

LINCOLN

Dearborn's premium make settled into a consistent and highly successful pattern after a turbulent ten years that had seen its evolution from stately flathead V-8 "bath-tub" (1950-51) through trim ohv V-8 performer (1952-55) to overblown cruiser (1956-59). Sales reflected the Sixties turn to predictable, tasteful luxury, increasing steadily each year to peak at 54,755 for 1966. It was not a postwar Lincoln record, however: That came in model-year 1949 with some 73,500 cars.

The 1960 line—Lincoln standard and Premiere series plus companion Continental Mark V models—was the last stand for the ambitious super-luxury program begun in 1956 with the limited-edition Mark II and a flashier, greatly enlarged Lincoln. The latter was quite successful, but the Mark II never sold as expected at its lofty $10,000 price. For 1958, Lincoln pinned its hopes on lower-priced Mark III sedans, hardtops, and convertibles, plus a near-identical group of Lincoln sedans and hardtops. All had massive new unit structures on a whopping 131-inch-wheelbase, plus a giant 430-cubic-inch V-8. Overall sales in that deep recession year were well down from 1957, though the Mark III sold far better than the II—enough to generate a profit, in fact, which was the whole idea.

This same fleet returned for '59, bolstered by a formal-roof limousine and a formal sedan for a renamed Mark IV line. Horsepower withered from 375 to 350 across the board. For 1960, the V-8 was further detuned to 315 bhp in a faint gesture to "economy," and the lineup repeated again, with the Marks being redesignated "V."

It bears mentioning that although the Mark II and 1958 Mark IIIs were products of a separate Continental Division (and thus "non-Lincolns"), later Marks and Continentals are properly regarded as Lincolns. This was largely due to the collapse of Ford's grand multi-divisional structure in the wake of the '58 recession and, in particular, the failure of Edsel to make its hoped-for sales impression in the medium-price field. Continental Division was thus duly merged with Lincoln after 1957; two years later, both Edsel and Mercury Divisions were folded in to form a short-lived M-E-L structure as a cost-cutting move. Ford's upper division then reverted to its original status as Lincoln-Mercury.

Following 1958-59, the standard 1960 Lincolns comprised a four-door sedan, hardtop coupe, and Landau hard-

1960 Continental Mark V convertible coupe

top sedan in base and somewhat plusher Premiere series. Four-doors were priced the same: $5441 and $5945, respectively, with hardtop coupes running about $250 less. Sitting some $900 above comparable Premieres were the mainstream Marks: a $6598 hardtop coupe, a four-door sedan and hardtop tagged at $6845, plus a $7058 convertible, still the division's sole soft-top. The formal sedan sold at $9208, the limousine at $10,230, but as might be expected, production remained minuscule: only about 170 units between them. Though the jumbo Marks never exceeded 13,000 in annual volume, they had their own special price niche, mid-way between Cadillac's Eldorados and long-wheelbase Sixty Specials, and they helped sales at a time when Lincoln sorely needed it.

Indeed, Lincoln's production total slipped for 1960, from just under 27,000 units to an even more dismal 24,820. In a way, this was curious. The national economy was still rebounding from '58, Lincoln prices had not risen appreciably, and standard equipment was as generous as ever, especially on Marks. The list ran to Twin-Range Turbo-Drive automatic, self-adjusting power brakes, power steering, heater/defroster, whitewall tires, undercoating, clock, windshield washers, radio, remote-control outside mirror, padded dash and sunvisors, back-up lights, parking brake warning light, and full wheel covers. Premieres added standard power seat and windows, while Marks sported leather upholstery.

The likely explanation for Lincoln's lackluster 1960 sales was a controversial and now-familiar basic design. Still

1960 Continental Mark V hardtop sedan

1961 Continental convertible sedan

1962 Continental convertible sedan

1964 Continental hardtop sedan

1965 Continental convertible sedan

1966 Continental four-door sedan

1967 Continental convertible sedan

massively square, it was again little changed for the second year in a row: just revised grilles and front bumpers (the latter's massive guards moving inboard of the odd, canted quad headlights), minor rear-end restyles, and, on Lincolns, a reworked rear roofline with an enlarged window, plus new full-length upper bodyside moldings. Despite appearances and 2½-ton curb weights, these cars remained surprisingly quick in a straight line and not that clumsy in the corners. But they were too big and ornate for a public that had suddenly turned against such excessive nonsense. Fortunately, Lincoln had prepared a far more appropriate and appealing car for 1961.

It was a totally redesigned "downsized" Lincoln Continental that replaced all the old behemoths with just two models: a thin-pillar four-door and America's first convertible sedan since the abortive Frazer Manhattan model of a decade before. Both rode a 123-inch wheelbase, the same as that of the trim mid-Fifties Lincolns, and featured a Thirties throwback in having rear doors hinged at the back, "suicide" style. Prices were in the middle of what had been Mark V territory: an announced $6067 for the hardtop and $6713 for the convertible.

Classic beauty and superb engineering made the '61 Lincoln the most satisfying since the magnificent prewar K-series—and one of the decade's most memorable cars. Enhancing both its image and sales was fortuitous timing, introduced just as a youthful and captivating First Family was occupying the White House. Continentals were soon seen in numerous newspaper and magazine photos as the transport of choice in the new administration, both personal and official, which is why these cars have since become known in some quarters as the "Kennedy Lincolns."

The '61's chiseled good looks resulted from the efforts of no fewer than seven Ford stylists—Eugene Bordinat, Don DeLaRossa, Elwood P. Engel, Gail L. Halderman, John Najjar, Robert M. Thomas, and George Walker—who were collectively honored with an award from the Industrial Design Institute. The IDI, which rarely bothers with automobiles, called the '61 Lincoln an "outstanding contribution of simplicity and design elegance." Interestingly, its basic cowl structure was shared with that year's revamped Thunderbird, which halved tooling costs for these two low-production cars, even though the Bird was very different aft of the cowl and on a 113-inch wheelbase.

With this car was introduced a basic Lincoln look that would continue into the late Eighties. The original was naturally the purest: smooth, gently curved bodysides topped by straight-through fenderlines edged in bright metal; a modest grille with horizontal quad headlamps outboard; a simple tail (not unlike the Mark II's) with a back panel repeating the grille theme; and taillamps set in the fender trailing edges. All corners were easily seen from behind the wheel, handy for parking. Side windows curved inward toward the top and were matched by a greenhouse with the greatest degree of "tumblehome" yet seen on a large American luxury car. Door glass would remain curved through '63, revert to flat for 1964-69, then become curved again. Unlike the old Frazer, the convertible sedan's side glass and window frames slid completely out of sight. So did its top, via 11 relays connecting mechanical and hydraulic linkages. (Much of its basic design, incidentally, stemmed from Ford's experience with the 1957-59 Skyliner retractable hardtops and 1958-60 T-Bird convertibles.)

Styling aside, these Lincolns were renowned for quality construction, thanks mostly to the efforts of Harold C. MacDonald, chief engineer of Ford's Car and Truck Group. The '61s had the most rigid unit body/chassis ever produced, the best sound insulation and shock damping in series production, extremely close machining tolerances for all mechanical components, an unprecedented number of long-life service components, a completely sealed electrical system, and superior rust and corrosion protection.

They were also the most thoroughly tested cars in Detroit history. Each engine—still the 430 V-8, albeit detuned to 300 bhp—was run on a dynamometer at 3500 rpm (equal to about 98 mph) for three hours, then torn down for inspection and reassembled. Automatic transmissions were tested for 30 minutes before installation. Each finished car was given a final 12-mile road test and checked for nearly 200 individual items, after which an ultraviolet light was used to visualize a fluorescent dye in lubricants as a check for leaks. Backing these measures was an unprecedented two-year, 24,000-mile warranty.

Response to the '61 line was immediate and satisfying. Sales exceeded 25,000 units, and Lincoln moved ahead of Chrysler's Imperial for keeps. Styling changes for the second and third year were minimal, Lincoln having promised that it would concentrate mainly on functional improvements, at least for a few years. A tidier grille with narrowed central crossbar and flush headlamps marked the '62s. The '63s had a finely checked grille, matching back-panel appliqué, and increased trunk space, plus engine tuning that yielded 20 additional horsepower.

Wheelbase grew to 126 inches for 1964, and would stay there through '69, but basic styling stayed the same. The main alterations aside from the aforementioned flat door glass were a slightly convex vertical-bar grille, broader rear window, and a lower-profile convertible top. The '65s received a horizontal grille motif, parking/turn signal lights in the front fenders, and ribbed taillights.

A body change for 1966 ushered in a revived two-door hardtop as Lincoln sought higher volume, the convertible having accounted for only ten percent of total sales. Body lines became less linear, a slight fender "hop-up" appearing just ahead of larger rear wheel cutouts. An extended front added about five inches to overall length, the grille acquired fine horizontal bars, and a bulged center section (carried through in sheetmetal above), and the front bumper wrapped all the way back to the front wheel openings. The V-8 was bored and stroked to 462 cid and 340 bhp.

With all this plus lower prices—as low as $5485 for the hardtop coupe—Lincoln sales reached nearly 55,000 for '66, though that was still only 25 percent of Cadillac's model-year volume. Another grille-and-taillight shuffle and a spring-loaded hood emblem appeared for '67, when the convertible sedan put in its final appearance and saw only 2276 copies. Overall production remained strong at more than 45,500.

The "Kennedy Lincoln" quickly became popular for con-

version into "commercial cars." Ford Motor Company probably started this ball rolling by building a brace of "White House convertible limousines" from 1961 models to replace the 1949-vintage Lincolns that had been in Presidential service since the Truman Administration. Striding a 156-inch wheelbase, these customs boasted six-piece roofs, with clear and opaque tops interchangeable in several configurations, plus retractable running boards for Secret Service agents and two-piece doors that allowed rear entry through a 15-inch-wide space. Also fitted were rear-facing aft-compartment jump seats, advanced communications gear, PA speaker, siren, emergency flashers, and numerous "classified" features. It was in one of these cars that President Kennedy made his fatal ride through Dallas on the afternoon of November 22, 1963.

After being updated with each year's Lincoln styling, both these Presidential limos were retired in October 1968 to be replaced by a current model. New features included a glass section above the main passenger compartment, with a hinged center that permitted occupants to stand up during a parade, and a rear bumper that could be lowered like an elevator as a platform for Secret Service agents. Security, communications, and engineering equipment was the most advanced of any automobile ever used by the White House. A similar car built from a '65 model ferried Pope Paul VI during his historic U.S. visit in October 1965.

Meantime, Lehmann-Peterson of Chicago crafted two Continental-based "Executive Limousines" in 1963, stretching the standard car 36 inches between wheel centers to a 159-inch dimension. The following year, with active support from Ford, L-P began offering a special-order 34-inch "stretch" of the longer-wheelbase '64 production model. Priced upwards of $15,000 and weighing 400-550 pounds more than showroom Lincolns, they continued to be built through decade's end, always with the appearance and feature changes of contemporary production models. Annual volume ranged from 15 to 130.

Lincoln's most intriguing development for 1968 was the return of the Continental Mark III. This was not a revival of the leviathan '58 but the lineal successor to the matchless 1956-57 Mark II. Predictably, it bore the personal stamp of company president Henry Ford II, just as his brother William had influenced the Mark II and their father Edsel had hatched the original 1940 "Mark I." Why "Mark III" instead of the expected "Mark VI?" Because HF II didn't view the heavyweight 1958-60 Mark III/IV/V as being true Continentals.

But this new one was, at least in spirit. It debuted in late 1968 as a personal-luxury car with long-hood/short-deck proportions in the classic Continental tradition. Styling was supervised by design chief Gene Bordinat, while Hermann Brunn, scion of the great coachbuilding family and a member of Bordinat's staff, was mainly responsible for the interior, endowing it with large, comfortable bucket seats and a woodgrained dash.

The result was a good-looking car with America's longest hood—more than six feet—and offered with a wide choice of luxury interiors and 26 exterior colors, including four special "Moondust" metallic paints. The 1969-71 models cost a bit more but were little changed otherwise.

1968 Continental hardtop coupe

1969 Continental hardtop coupe

1969 Continental Mark III hardtop coupe

Standard equipment ran to Select-Shift Turbo-Drive automatic, power brakes (discs in front, drums in the rear), concealed headlights, ventless side windows, power seats and windows, flow-through ventilation, and 150 pounds of sound insulation.

Arriving at a reasonable $6585, this Mark III was actually a structural cousin to the new-for-'67 Thunderbird sedan, set on the same 117.2-inch wheelbase (some nine inches shorter than the Mark II's). Overall length was identical with that of Cadillac's front-drive Eldorado (another

'67 newcomer). Power came from a new 460-cid V8—one of Detroit's largest—with 10.5:1 compression and 365 bhp. Also adopted for the standard '68 Continentals, it would remain Lincoln's mainstay powerplant for the next ten years.

Because of its late introduction (in April), the Mark III saw only 7770 units for model-year '68. But there was no question about its correctness for the market: More than 23,000 would be sold for '69, another 21,500 for 1970, and over 27,000 for '71. The rival front-drive Eldorado may have been more technically advanced, but the Mark clearly had its own appeal, for it nearly matched the Eldo in sales each year through 1971 (save for '70, when the Mark lagged by about 7400 units). This was a significant achievement considering that Lincoln's annual production had never come close to Cadillac's.

Still with their '66 bodyshells, the '67 Continental sedan and hardtop received a new horizontal-texture grille and matching rear panel appliqué, plus a large "star" nose ornament. For 1968, a multi-function lamp at each corner provided a cleaner look by combining turn signals, side markers (newly required by Washington), parking lamps (front), and brake and taillights (rear). Model-year volume for this line totaled a bit over 39,000.

Announcing the '69s was a finely checked grille newly separated from the headlamps, but still with a raised center section extending into the hood. Wheelbase was untouched, though overall length was now up to 225.4 inches. A new Town Car interior option for the sedan provided "unique, super-puff leather-and-vinyl seats and door panels, luxury wood-tone front seatback and door trim inserts, extra plush carpeting, and special napped nylon headlining." Additional safety equipment introduced per governmental decree included dual-circuit brake system with warning light, four-way emergency flasher, day/night rearview mirror, and energy-absorbing steering column and instrument panel. Production eased once again, settling at about 38,300.

By decade's end, the original "Kennedy" Continental had grown appreciably in size, if not weight, but sales were always good and occasionally great, for the cars won many friends among luxury buyers. Performance was always respectable, too, with a typical 0-60 of 11 seconds and top speed of up to 115 mph. Clean design, careful attention to quality, and conservative but thorough engineering had resulted in highly desirable luxury automobiles, not to mention a highly successful, reborn Mark series. Both would enjoy even greater popularity in later years.

LINCOLN AT A GLANCE, 1960-1969										
	1960	1961	1962	1963	1964	1965	1966	1967	1968	1969
Price Range, $	5253-10,230	6069-6715	6074-6720	6270-6916	6292-6938	6292-6938	5485-6383	5553-6449	5736-6585	5830-6758
Weight Range, lbs.	4917-5500	4927-5215	4966-5370	4936-5340	5055-5393	5075-5475	4985-5480	4940-5505	4739-4978	4762-5005
Wheelbases, in.	131	123	123	123	126	126	126	126	117.2-126	117.2-126
8 Cyl. Engines, hp	315	300	300	320	320	320	340	340	365	365

MERCURY

Mercury's road in the Sixties runs through a maze of sizes and body styles, plus some erratic and usually confusing uses of certain model names. Yet the make's fortunes generally tended upward, and some names were consistent. Comet and Monterey, for example, spanned the entire decade, while Montclair and Park Lane appeared only on big Mercs through 1968. Meteor, long used on a special Ford-based Canadian line, came south for two very different U.S. applications between 1961 and '63.

The Mercury names most familiar at decade's dawn were Monterey, Montclair, and Park Lane, which again graced 126-inch-wheelbase giants. These had been totally redesigned for 1959, and might also have been offered as Edsels had things gone better with that ill-starred '58 newcomer. Still, with huge compound-curve windshields and two-ton curb weights, these biggest of the "Big Ms" were handsomely facelifted for 1960, losing a little chrome while gaining a tidier new concave grille and more discreet "gull-wing" rear-end treatment. Model choices were mostly as before: Cruiser two- and four-door hardtops in each series, four-door Monterey/Montclair sedans, Monterey two-door sedan, Park Lane convertible, and, still in a separate series, four-door Commuter and wood-sided Colony Park hardtop wagons.

Engine choices remained at three, all big-block V-8s with slightly reduced power (via lowered compression) to appease buyers made mileage-minded by the '58 recession. A 312-cubic-incher with 205 horsepower was standard for Monterey and Commuter, an optional 383 brought 280 horses, and the 310-bhp Lincoln 430 was standard for other offerings. Model year production rose slightly from '59 to some 155,000, but the gain wasn't that impressive, all things considered.

The "Big M" shrunk noticeably in both size and price for 1961. In fact, it was again basically a "deluxe Ford," though on an inch-longer 120-inch wheelbase. Thus ended four years of unique Mercury chassis and bodyshells, reflecting the collapse of Dearborn's grand mid-Fifties "divisionalization" plan, the attempt at a GM-style five-make corporate line that had also spawned Edsel. Much-reduced sales since 1957 had rendered tooling costs for a separate platform unacceptably high, hence the return to Mercury's original 1939 concept.

With this came the first American Meteor, two- and four-door sedans and hardtops offered in 600 and nicer 800 series for vastly reduced prices beginning at $2535. In effect, these filled the gap left by Edsel's termination the previous year. Monterey was now the premium line, offering four-door sedan and hardtop, two-door hardtop, and convertible. Wagons, still a separate series but now conventional pillared four-doors, expanded to six- and nine-passenger Commuters and Colony Parks. Styling was even more conservative than in 1960. The grille was still concave, but flanks were newly rounded and Fifties gimmicks consigned to history. Standard on Meteor and Monterey was a 175-bhp 292 V-8, though a 223 Ford six with 135-bhp was available as an economical alternative on Meteors. Across-the-board options included a 220-bhp 352 and new big-block 390s with 300/330 bhp. Although Meteor actually outsold Monterey, sales were not spectacular. Accord-

1960 Montclair Cruiser hardtop sedan

1960 Comet four-door sedan

1961 Monterey convertible coupe

1962 Meteor Custom two-door sedan

1962 Monterey Custom S-55 convertible coupe

63

1963 Monterey Custom S-55 hardtop coupe

1963 Meteor S-33 hardtop coupe

1964 Park Lane convertible coupe

1964 Comet Cyclone hardtop coupe

ingly, the line was replaced for '62 by a "Monterey 6" and the name moved to Mercury's version of the new intermediate Ford Fairlane.

Most everything recorded about the 1962-63 Fairlane (see Ford) applies to this second Meteor. Styling was busier and model names were different, but most everything else was shared. That included powertrains, namely Ford's fine new small-block V-8 with 221 cid and 145 bhp or 260 cid and 164 bhp. Custom denoted upmarket Meteors, S-33 the

sportier bucket-seaters (a two-door sedan for '62, a hardtop coupe for '63). Station wagons—woody-look Country Cruiser and plain-sided base and Custom—joined two hardtops as new for 1963. For all this, the mid-size Meteor didn't sell nearly as well as Fairlane, and Mercury dropped it for 1964 in favor of an extensively upgraded Comet.

Also once planned as an Edsel, the first Comet was basically Ford's hugely successful new 1960 Falcon with squared-up roofline, a double-row concave grille, and an extended stern with canted fins and oval taillamps. Wheelbase was 114 inches on two- and four-door sedans; wagons used Falcon's 109.5-inch span. It wasn't exciting, but it sold well: over 116,000 for the abbreviated debut season. Sales set a record for '61 at 197,000 units and were strong for '62, which hurt Meteor. In fact, one reason Meteor didn't sell well is that Comet was comparably sized yet less expensive. Mercury was wise to make Comet its only small car after '63. Sales jumped by 55,000 units for '64 and remained high into '67.

Though more elaborately trimmed, early Comets were priced less than $100 above comparable Falcons. S-22, a $2300 bucket-seat two-door sedan, responded to the sporty-compact craze beginning in 1961, when all Comets gained an optional 101-bhp six. Custom sedans and wagons and a posh Villager wagon with imitation tree trim aided '62 sales. The following year brought Custom and S-22 convertibles and Sportster hardtop coupes. A squarish facelift arrived for 1964, when S-22 was renamed Caliente, and any Comet could be ordered with the outstanding 260 small-block. A mid-season Caliente offshoot, a hardtop called Cyclone, offered even higher performance from a standard 210-bhp 289.

Comet received its first major overhaul for 1966, shifting from compact to intermediate size by adopting that year's sleek new Fairlane shell. This underlined a basic marketing decision: Mercury customers were assumed to be wealthier than Ford buyers, and thus likely happier with a compact larger than Falcon.

Comet retained this 116-inch-wheelbase platform through 1969, but sales waned along with the name, which by 1967 mostly applied to a pair of very basic "202" sedans. Filling out that year's line were Capri, Caliente, Cyclone, and Station Wagon. All were swept away for 1968 by a three-series Montego line on the same wheelbase: base sedan and hardtop coupe; MX sedan, hardtop, convertible, and wagon; and top-line MX Brougham sedan and hardtop, the last boasting high-quality cloth interior and other luxuries. The Comet name was retained for a price-leader hardtop, then was temporarily shelved after 1969.

Mercury jumped into the mid-size muscle market with both feet and won more than a few racing laurels. For 1966, it brought out a smoothly styled new Cyclone GT hardtop coupe and convertible powered by Ford's 335-bhp 390 V-8 and offered with a variety of useful suspension upgrades. The '67 was even more thrilling, with optional 427 big-blocks delivering 410-425 bhp.

Similar street racers were available for '68, though the 427 was detuned to 390 bhp. Besides Montego, the mid-size line included new base and GT Cyclone hardtop coupes with the same curvy new lower-body contours and racy, full-fastback rooflines *à la* Ford Mustang/Torino. There was also a one-year-only GT notchback. For 1969, Mercury unleashed the Cyclone CJ with Ford's 428 big-block Cobra Jet mill. GTs and CJs had black grilles, special emblems, bodyside paint stripes, and unique rear-end styling. CJs carried a functional hood scoop when equipped with optional Ram-Air induction. Though Ford won the 1968-69 NASCAR championship, Cyclones turned in the most notable performances. A highlight was Cale Yarborough's win in the '68 Daytona 500 at an average 143.25 mph.

For all its activity in compacts and intermediates, big cars remained Mercury's bread-and-butter throughout the Sixties. Annual production ran around 100,000 units except for record back-to-back performances in 1965-66—over 165,000 each year. Of all the big Mercs, only Monterey stayed the entire decade. The upper-echelon Montclair and Park Lane, dropped for '61, returned for 1964-68, then vanished again, replaced by the Marquis line.

With Meteor an intermediate, the 1962 full-size line was regrouped into Monterey, Monterey Custom, and Station Wagon series, with the convertible shifting to the upper-priced Custom group. Joining the bucket-seat brigade at midyear were the S-55 hardtop coupe and convertible. Styling was busier, with tunneled taillights and a complex convex grille. All previous V-8s returned, as did the faithful big six as standard power for base Montereys and Commuter wagons.

A similar array on the same 120-inch wheelbase returned for 1963, when a heavy reskin introduced "Breezeway Styling" for non-wagon closed models: reverse-slant rear windows that dropped down for ventilation as on the old Turnpike Cruiser (and 1958-60 Continental Marks). Wagons were trimmed to a pair of Colony Parks. Joining the S-55 sub-series at midyear was a handsome "slantback" two-door hardtop like Ford's. Engines were again all V-8s: 390s with 250-330 bhp, a new 406-cid extension packing 385/405 bhp, and as a late-season option, a bored-out high-performance 427 with 410 bhp.

Tradition returned for silver anniversary 1964 with a four-series line: Monterey, Montclair, Park Lane, and Commuter/Colony Park wagons. The first three included Breezeway two- and four-door hardtops and four-door sedans (Montereys still included a pillared two-door), plus slantback "Marauder" hardtop coupes and sedans. A toothy convex grille replaced the concave '63 affair, and trim was shuffled. The previous 390 V-8s continued, but the 406s didn't, giving way completely to 427s with 410/425 optional bhp for all models save wagons. Big-inch Marauders were awesome performers.

Record 1965 brought a larger full-size body with crisp, linear styling "in the Lincoln Continental tradition," as well as a new "Torque Box" frame (tuned for each body to minimize noise, vibration, and harshness). Wagons now rode the 119-inch Ford wheelbase; other models were up to 123. Breezeways thinned to a trio of four-door sedans, all hardtops were now slantbacks, and the Marauder name was played down amid calls for greater automotive safety. V-8s were now a quartet of 390s with 250-330 bhp and a lone 425-bhp 427. The basic '65 look carried into 1966 with a

1965 Park Lane hardtop sedan

1966 S-55 convertible coupe

1967 Cougar XR-7 hardtop coupe

1967 Comet Cyclone GT hardtop coupe

1968 Cougar XR-7 hardtop coupe

65

new die-cast grille and, on hardtop coupes, a "sweep-style roof" with concave backlight.

More rounded bodysides mixed well with sharp-edged fenders for '67. Sedans adopted conventional rooflines but still offered the drop-down rear window as an option. Hardtop coupes received "faster" profiles. Two new limited-production line-toppers bowed: Marquis, a two-door hardtop with broad rear pillars and standard vinyl roof covering, and the similar Park Lane Brougham hardtop sedan, which expanded into a complete series the following year. Intermediates were waging Mercury's sporty-car wars, so the bucket-seat S-55 convertible and hardtop were in their final year, and now just a Monterey option package. Respective production was minuscule: just 145 and 570.

After a minor '68 facelift, the big Mercs were fully revised for 1969. Wheelbases grew to 121 inches on wagons and 124 inches on other models, sizes that would persist until their first downsizing of 1979. Series regrouped around base Monterey, revived Monterey Custom, and a full Marquis line, which included Colony Park wagon, convertible, and standard, along with Brougham sedans,

1969 Cougar Eliminator hardtop coupe

1969 Cyclone Spoiler fastback hardtop coupe

hardtop coupes, and hardtop sedans. Riding the shorter wheelbase was a new Marauder, a high-performance "tunnelback" hardtop that garnered 14,666 sales. Offered in standard and spiffier X-100 trim, it shared the Marquis' hidden-headlamp front and the ventless side glass used by most other models. V-8s comprised the usual 390s and a new 429 big-block with 360 bhp, the latter standard for Marader X-100, optional elsewhere.

One of Mercury's most interesting and desirable Sixties products was the Cougar, an upscale edition of Ford's highly successful Mustang "ponycar," premiering for 1967 as a lone two-door hardtop in two basic permutations. Convertibles were added for 1969. Striding a three-inch-longer wheelbase than Mustang (111 in all), Cougar offered more luxury and standard power for about $200 additional. Mustang's base engine was a six, Cougar's a 200-bhp 289 V-8. The big 335-bhp 428 CJ became an extra-cost option for 1969-70.

The first Cougars arguably looked best, with hidden headlamps in an "electric-shaver" grille and a matching back panel with sequential turn signals, a gimmick borrowed from Ford's Thunderbird. Length and width increased on the '69s, which sported Buick-like sweepspear bodyside contours, ventless side glass, less distinctive "faces," and full-width taillights. The most luxurious Cougars would always be tagged XR-7. For 1967-68, this meant a rich interior with leather accents and full instrumentation in a simulated walnut dashboard. A separate GT package delivered a firmed-up suspension for more capable roadholding and a standard 320-bhp 390 V-8 for extra go. For 1968 came a GTE edition with several unique appearance features and a 390-bhp 427. The hottest 1969 Cougar was the Eliminator hardtop, with 428 power and standard rear-deck spoiler. Convertibles saw very low production, as would all ragtop Cougars.

Though it never approached Mustang in sales, Cougar was more solid and elegant, yet just as roadable. And production was more than respectable, starting at 150,000 units and not dropping below 100,000 through '69.

Cougar put the finishing touch on a decade that saw Mercury begin to rival Lincoln in the luxury field while rejuvenating the performance image it had enjoyed in the late Forties and early Fifties. But though the Mercury lineup would remain varied, and even expand into subcompacts, its various members would become increasingly like equivalent Fords until the one real distinction became styling that attempted a closer tie-in with Lincoln's.

MERCURY AT A GLANCE, 1960-1969										
	1960	1961	1962	1963	1964	1965	1966	1967	1968	1969
Price Range, $	1998-4018	2000-3191	2084-3738	2084-3900	2126-3549	2154-3599	2206-3614	2284-3989	2477-3888	2532-4262
Weight Range, lbs.	2399-4558	2376-4171	2420-4198	2462-4318	2539-4287	2584-4263	2779-4383	2787-4297	2982-4331	3060-4436
Wheelbases, in.	109.5-126	109.5-120	109.5-120	109.5-120	109.5-120	109.5-123	113-123	111-123	111-123	111-124
6 Cyl. Engines, hp	90	85-135	85-138	85-101	101-116	120	120	120	115	155
8 Cyl. Engines, hp	205-310	175-330	145-385	145-410	164-425	200-425	200-345	200-425	195-390	220-360

1961 1500 convertible

1961 1500 convertible

The whimsical Metropolitan is really a car of the Fifties—indeed, it originated in the late Forties—and the few that sold in the Sixties seemed out of place. Approved for production in 1952-53 and facelifted for the first and only time in 1956, it was a tad awkward on its stubby 85-inch wheelbase, especially with Detroit styling that strained to echo traits of later Nash models (the last of which was built in 1957).

But the Met appealed greatly to those who needed no more than two seats and space for a few grocery bags. Besides, it was cute—if in an ugly sort of way. Only 52 horsepower was available from its 91-cubic-inch four-cylinder engine, but that could see the 1900-pound runabout up to 70 miles an hour. More importantly, it gave the Met impressive fuel economy: up to 40 miles per gallon. Such attributes were valuable in America's small-car awakening of the late Fifties/early Sixties. Metropolitan registrations, which had rarely exceeded 10,000 units a year through 1956, broke 15,000 in '57, then surged to 22,000 in '59, though that would be the peak. American Motors was mainly concerned with Ramblers by then, but was sufficiently impressed by Met sales to continue imports for a few more years.

The Met was born in the early postwar period when Nash-Kelvinator president George Mason, a small-car fanatic, became interested in a tiny prototype car by freelance designer Bill Flajole. This was quickly developed into Nash's experimental NXI, which generated encouraging public reaction. For various reasons, Mason thought the car should be built in Europe for export to America, where he judged it could make a modest profit. After talking to Triumph and Morris in England, he contracted with Austin for the powerplant; Birmingham coachbuilders Fisher & Ludlow were signed to supply bodywork. Completed shells (unitized per Nash/AMC practice) went to Austin for drive-

train installation and final assembly before shipment to the States.

There was no change whatsoever in the Metropolitan during 1960-62. The only version available was the updated 1500 model introduced in 1956. Prices in these final years were $1673 for the hardtop version or $1697 for the soft-top convertible. A $53 surcharge was levied for West Coast delivery in 1962-63.

What finished off the Metropolitan was the dual onslaught of the German Volkswagen and American compacts. The prewar-designed Beetle had proved its worth by 1961 and was still gaining in sales, while Detroit's larger, recently issued compacts offered space for five and lots of luggage, plus prices within $200 of the Met's. American Motors itself hastened the Met's demise by reviving the original 100-inch-wheelbase Rambler (as the 1958-60 American) and selling it for only some $125 more than the import.

As a result, Met sales fell fast, and production was halted in mid-1960, though close to 1300 leftovers were retailed and registered as 1961-62 models. American Motors kept only annual registration figures, which may or may not coincide with model-year production: 13,103 for 1960; 853 for '61; and 412 for '62.

METROPOLITAN AT A GLANCE, 1960-1962			
	1960	**1961**	**1962**
Price Range, $	1673-1697	1673-1697	1673-1697
Weight Range, lbs.	1850-1890	1850-1890	1850-1890
Wheelbases, in.	85	85	85
4 Cyl. Engines, hp	52	52	52

OLDSMOBILE

Like other makers, Oldsmobile responded to a fast-fragmenting Sixties market with a variety of new models, most of which sold very well. Olds never fell below seventh in industry output during these years and often ran fourth, rising from about 347,000 cars for 1960 to 635,000 at decade's end. Jumping on the 1961 bandwagon for upscale compacts, Olds fielded the F-85, which, together with its later Cutlass variations, saw progressively higher annual production through 1968. This reflected an astute matching of customer tastes with new products: small V-8s for 1961-62, larger compacts with available V-6 for 1964-65, and the high-performance 4-4-2 series from 1964. Each year's junior Olds line was invariably right on the money. The division's standard-size cars also sold consistently well.

The F-85 was one of GM's "second-wave" compacts, along with the Buick Special and Pontiac Tempest. All were evolved from Chevy's rear-engine 1960 Corvair, with the same basic "Y-body" platform, albeit reworked for an orthodox front-engine/rear-drive format. Tempest, with its curved driveshaft and rear transaxle, was the most radical of the B-O-P trio. Special and F-85 were more conventional. The latter two were powered by the all-new, all-aluminum, Buick-built V-8 of 215 cubic inches and 155 horsepower, which gave them reasonable go (typical 0-60 mph: 13 seconds) and economy (18 mpg). In appearance, the Olds was a bit cleaner than the Buick, with a simpler front end (a small-scale rendition of that year's big-Olds face) but the same sculptured bodysides and crisp roofline.

Naming the F-85 had presented a bit of a problem. Starfire was the first choice, but it had been used before on the mammoth 1954-57 Ninety-Eight convertibles, and was therefore deemed inappropriate for this small, sporty car. (Besides, a somewhat different Starfire had been planned for '61.) "Rockette" was nixed because it projected an unwanted image of the Radio City Music Hall dancers. The

1960 98 Celebrity four-door sedan

final choice looked to the Corvette-like F-88 show car of 1954, with "85" selected to avoid confusion with big 88s. F-85s were initially offered as four-door sedans, pillared club coupes, and hatchback four-door wagons in standard and Deluxe trim, all on a 112-inch wheelbase. The Deluxe coupe with bucket seats and luxury appointments was called Cutlass, a name that would eventually supplant F-85. Plain and Cutlass convertibles arrived for 1962.

All '62 Cutlasses came with a 185-bhp "Power-Pack" V-8, but greater interest surrounded a new companion model: the turbocharged Jetfire hardtop coupe, sharing honors with that year's new Chevy Corvair Monza Spyder as America's first high-volume turbocars. The blower lifted V-8 output to 215 bhp—one horsepower per cubic inch—though carbon buildup with certain grades of gas prompted the addition of an unusual water injection system (actually, a water/alcohol mix). While the Jetfire was remarkably fast (0-60 mph: about 8.5 seconds; top speed: 107 mph), the injection system proved unreliable. For 1964, Olds abandoned turbos for a conventional 330-cid V-8 of 230-290 bhp and made Buick's new 155-bhp 225-cid V-6 base power for the F-85 line. The latter ran unchanged until 1966, when an inline six of the same horsepower was substituted.

1960 Super 88 convertible coupe

1961 Super 88 Starfire convertible coupe

1962 F-85 Deluxe Jetfire convertible coupe

The compact Oldsmobiles grew to intermediate size after 1963, GM taking note of the huge sales generated by Ford's Fairlane since '62. Wheelbase went to 115 inches for '64, when Holiday hardtop coupes were added; for '68, the line was split, with a 112-inch span on two-door models and a 116-inch platform for four-doors. Styling actually improved over time. The original 1961-62 design was made more "important" for '63. The '64 was bulkier but still very clean and had an even closer resemblance to the big Oldsmobiles. Straight beltlines yielded to more flowing "Coke-bottle" contours for '66, when models again expanded via hardtop sedans in Cutlass and F-85 Deluxe trim. Appearance began to clutter up again after '68, with busier grilles and sometimes clumsy vinyl tops.

The most exciting F-85s were called 4-4-2, which meant four speeds (400 cubic inches after '65), four-barrel carburetor, and dual exhausts. The debut 1964 edition was a package option for the Cutlass coupe, convertible, and hardtop coupe comprising 310-bhp 330 V-8, heavy-duty suspension, and four-speed manual gearbox. The '65 was hotter still with a 345-bhp 400 (a debored version of the full-size cars' then-new 425 V-8), plus heavy-duty shocks, springs, rear axle, driveshaft, engine mounts, steering, and frame; stabi-

lizer bars front and rear; fat tires; special exterior and interior trim; 11-inch clutch; and a 70-amp battery—all for about $250. Performance was sensational: 0-60 in 7.5 seconds, the standing quarter-mile in 17 seconds at 85 mph, top speed of 125 mph. The 4-4-2 proved, as *Motor Trend* magazine said, "that Detroit can build cars that perform, handle and stop, without sacrificing road comfort. . . ."

Each year's 4-4-2 was eagerly awaited. Though the 400 V-8 was never pushed much beyond 350 bhp, Oldsmobile's muscle cars remained handsome, fast, and fun—better balanced overall than most competitors, which had too much power for their chassis. The '69s sported big 4-4-2 numerals on front fenders, rear deck, and body-color vertical grille divider; black grille finish; and a unique "bi-level" hood with special contrasting paint stripes. If a bit outlandish, it was no less the performance car it had been in the beginning.

Arriving for 1966 was the most innovative Olds in a generation: the intriguing front-wheel-drive Toronado. Offered only as a hardtop coupe on a 119-inch wheelbase, it represented a clean break with the past—and a commitment to front drive that GM would embrace company-wide by 1980. It was a big turnabout for a company that had once panned the front-drive Cord, but GM had planned it well.

1962 Starfire hardtop coupe

1963 F-85 Deluxe Jetfire hardtop coupe

1963 Starfire convertible coupe

1964 98 hardtop coupe

1964 Cutlass 442 Holiday hardtop coupe

1965 98 Luxury Sedan

1966 Cutlass 442 convertible coupe

1966 Toronado hardtop coupe

1967 98 Holiday hardtop coupe

The goal for Toronado was traditional American power combined with outstanding handling and traction. Its 425 V-8 was shared with the conventional full-size models (but delivered an extra 10 horsepower—385 total) and teamed with a new "split" automatic transmission. A torque converter mounted behind the engine connected via chain drive and sprocket to a self-shifting Turbo Hydra-Matic transmission located remotely under the left cylinder bank. The chain drive, flexible yet virtually unbreakable, saved weight and cut costs. It also resulted in a very compact drivetrain that opened up extra cabin room. Most previous front-drive systems had put the engine behind a front-mounted transmission. Toronado's split transmission allowed the engine to be placed directly over the front wheels for a front/rear weight distribution of 54/46 percent—good for a big front-driver that some said would never work well simply because it was so big and heavy (over 4300 pounds at the curb).

Toronado styling was as sophisticated as its engineering. The C-pillars spilled gently down from the roof, there was no beltline "break" behind the rear side windows, the rakish fastback roofline terminated in a neatly cropped tail, the curved fuselage was set off by boldly flared wheel arches, and there was a distinctive front end with hidden headlamps. *Automobile Quarterly* editor Don Vorderman termed the result "logical, imaginative, and totally unique."

It was just as superb on the road. Understeer wasn't excessive for a front-driver, it ran quietly at 100 mph, and top speed was near 135 mph. Unquestionably, Toronado was the most outstanding single Olds of this decade. Too bad the 1968-70 versions weren't as clean as the 1966-67. Both looked heavier in front, gaining a simple but massive combination bumper/grille, while the '69 grew longer via extra rear-end sheetmetal that was tacked on in an apparent effort to create a more conventional notchback profile.

Despite the likes of Toronado and 4-4-2, big cars remained Oldsmobile's stock-in-trade during the Sixties. The 1960 models were basically the expansive new "Linear Look" '59s with simpler, more dignified lines courtesy of a below-the-belt reskin. Pointy "rocket" rear fenders and busier bodysides marked the '61s, followed by more involved grilles and rear-end treatments for '62. Wheelbases and series remained the same as for '59: a 123-inch span for price-leader Dynamic 88 and extra-performance Super 88 as well as a 126.5-inch dimension for the luxury 98 (increasingly written as "Ninety Eight"). A 1961 newcomer was the bucket-seat Starfire convertible on the Super 88 chassis. A companion hardtop coupe was added for '62, when both were put into a separate series.

Further line expansion occurred for 1964, when the Dynamic moved up a notch in price to make room for new Jetstar 88s. Among them was a bucket-seat Jetstar I sports coupe with concave backlight à la Pontiac's contemporary Grand Prix, but the Olds didn't catch on and was dropped after only two years. Super 88 was renamed Delta 88 for 1965; two years later, Dynamic and Jetstar were consolidated into a similar Delmont 88 line. This remained Oldsmobile's full-size "family" fleet until 1969, when standard, Custom, and Royale Deltas appeared on a 124-inch wheelbase. That year's 98 moved up to a 127-inch platform.

Despite body changes for '65 and '69, big-Olds styling maintained a consistent look. A "dumbbell" grille shape persisted through 1966, after which the first of Oldsmobile's now-familiar split grilles appeared. Lines were crisp, straight, and simple for 1963-64, progressively curvier and bulkier thereafter. Body styles were the usual assortment through '63, after which wagons were dropped in deference to F-85/Cutlass-based Fiesta and Vista Cruiser models, the latter arriving with a raised, glassed-in upper rear superstructure (shared by Buick's contemporary Skylark-based Sportwagons). For 1966, Olds cheated a line of Vista Cruisers, a separate series of conventional and high-top models on a special 120-inch wheelbase that grew to 121 for 1968.

After a carryover 1960, power for large Oldsmobiles through 1963 was provided by a 394 V-8 (a heavily reworked version of the division's original 1949 "Rocket," new for '59) delivering 250 bhp in base 88s, and up to 345 bhp in the '62 Starfire. The low-priced '64 Jetstar shared the F-85's 330 engine. For 1965, the 394 was stroked out to 425 cid, and power rose gradually, reaching 375 bhp by 1967.

The following year brought a still longer stroke for a massive 455 cid but only 365 bhp, the power being lost to the advent of emission controls and necessary detuning. The '67 Delmont offered both the 425 and 330 engines. The latter was bored out to 350 cid and 250 bhp for 1968.

Of Oldsmobile's two big bucket-seat performance cars, only the Starfire had any success. Early models sported broad sweeps of brushed aluminum outside, while luxurious interiors with bucket seats and center console were hallmarks throughout. Despite fairly stiff prices in the $4000-$5000 range, sales zoomed, from 7600 for debut '61 to over 40,000 for '62. But that would be the peak, demand tapering off quickly through the end of the series in 1966 (the convertible departed the year before). Jetstar I was the same idea at a more popular price—around $3600 base—but only some 22,600 were called for over two model years. Though neither was anything like a true sports car despite Oldsmobile's claims to the contrary, they were distinctive and handled well for their size. Today, they rate with 4-4-2s and Toronados as the most collectible Oldsmobiles of this decade.

1968 442 Holiday hardtop coupe

1969 Toronado hardtop coupe

1969 Delta 88 Royale Holiday hardtop coupe

1969 98 Luxury Sedan

OLDSMOBILE AT A GLANCE, 1960-1969										
	1960	1961	1962	1963	1964	1965	1966	1967	1968	1969
Price Range, $	2835-4362	2330-4647	2403-4744	2403-4742	2343-4753	2344-4778	2348-4812	2512-4945	2512-4750	2561-5030
Weight Range, lbs.	4026-4506	2541-4445	2599-4428	2599-4367	2824-4337	2940-4286	2951-4366	3062-4374	3062-4278	3082-4368
Wheelbases, in.	123-126	112-126	112-126	112-126	115-126	115-126	115-126	115-126	112-126	112-127
6 Cyl. Engines, hp					155	155	155	155	155	155
8 Cyl. Engines, hp	240-315	155-330	155-345	155-345	230-345	250-370	250-385	250-385	250-400	250-400

PLYMOUTH

Plymouth had plenty of ups-and-downs in the Fifties—and would have plenty more in the Sixties. Long the industry's number-three seller behind Chevrolet and Ford, Plymouth again ran third for 1959 with some 458,000 cars, but after '60 wouldn't hold that spot again for another 11 years. For 1960, volume eased to just under 448,000 despite sales support from the all-new Valiant compact. By 1962, Chrysler Corporation's breadwinner had dropped all the way back to eighth, knocked out by Rambler, Pontiac, and Oldsmobile—as well as its own slow-selling line of smaller big cars with no full-size alternatives. Despite a modest recovery that was completed by '65, Plymouth would not be able to dislodge Pontiac from third through decade's end, finishing fourth every year from 1963.

Trouble was apparent in 1960's "Unibody" line of garishly redesigned standard models, still on the 118-inch wheelbase of 1957-59 and arrayed in Savoy, Belvedere, Fury, and separate Suburban wagon series. "Misshapen" may best describe the styling, with tailfins that strained to mimic the outlandish appendages of '59 Cadillacs.

But there was good news in a new 225-cubic-inch slant six with 145 horsepower, replacing the old Plymouth L-head as base power at last. It was a fine engine, exceptionally strong and reliable, and would be a corporate mainstay for over 20 years. Plymouth's 1960 V-8s were largely '59 reruns, all "wedgeheads": 318s with 230/260 bhp for Savoys and low-line wagons; 361s delivering 260/305/310 bhp in Belvederes and mid-line Suburbans; and top-dog "Golden Commando" 383 with ram-induction and 325/330 bhp for Furys and Sport Suburbans. Though Rambler's more conservative styling and even thriftier sixes scored 2000 more units for calendar 1960, Plymouth won the model-year race by a substantial 25,000-plus.

But the standard Plymouths were again drastically restyled for 1961, suddenly shorn of fins but still plenty weird thanks to a new pinched grille and ponderous bullet taillights. Furys mercifully lost their extra-cost "toilet seats"—the simulated rear-deck spare-tire outlines so beloved of Chrysler design chief Virgil Exner (as introduced with the '57 Imperial). V-8s were reshuffled. The '61 361 V-8 was cut to 305/310-bhp offerings, a third 383 bowed with 340 bhp, and Chrysler's biggest, the mighty 413 wedge, came to Plymouth with 350/375 bhp. But the odd "plucked chicken" styling combined with still-deteriorating workmanship to boost Rambler into third, Plymouth dropping to fourth on model-year volume that just managed to break 350,000.

1960 Fury hardtop sedan

1960 Valiant four-door sedan

Then, Plymouth made its worst mistake of the decade. Anticipating strong demand for smaller "standards," Exner sliced wheelbases by eight inches, trimmed curb weights by 550 pounds, and applied strange, Valiant-like styling to a 1962 lineup unchanged save for a bucket-seat convertible and hardtop coupe called Sport Fury (a name resurrected from '59). The result was a fleet of lighter, more maneuverable Plymouths that could get away with a smaller standard engine: the 225 slant six, of course. Previous V-8 selections returned, now all options. The larger ones were more potent. The 361 went to 310 bhp, the 383 to 330/335, and the big 413 to 365/380. The ultimate 413 was a 410-bhp job that made these Plymouths (and sister Dodges) the cars to beat on quarter-mile tracks. But mainstream buyers, not enthusiasts, were what mattered, and they still hungered for "full-size" cars. Not surprisingly, Ford and Chevrolet prospered while Plymouth sank to eighth in model-year output with less than 340,000 units. At least that would be the decade low.

Beating a hasty retreat, Plymouth issued more conservative, squared-up styling for '63, then a Chevy-like '64 facelift, both crafted under Ford alumnus Elwood Engel, who replaced Exner in 1962. But this didn't help much, either. Plymouth's 1963 rebound to fourth came mainly on continuing strong demand for compact Valiants rather than sizable gains in its standard-car sales.

Engines in these years stood pretty much pat save a notable '63 newcomer. This was the wedgehead 426, a bored-out 413 with ultra-high compression—from 11:1 up to 13.5:1—packing 370/375 bhp with twin four-barrel carburetors or 415/425 with ram induction. Richard Petty gave Plymouth morale a big boost by winning the '64 NASCAR championship hands down, driving a Fury hardtop whose new "slantback" rear roofline undoubtedly aided aerodynamics on the long-distance "supertracks." But Petty's triumph came with a 426 *hemi-head* V-8 available only to

1960 Fury convertible coupe

racers, not the general public. Still, it was heartening to see Chrysler's famed Fifties muscle mill revived for a new "horsepower race" that was already well underway.

A full-scale Plymouth renaissance was well underway by 1965, mostly because of that year's return to the full-size fold with big, blocky Furys on a new 119-inch wheelbase (121 inches for wagons). Fury I and II offered two sedans and a wagon; Fury III added two hardtops and a convertible; at the top were a bucket-seat Sport Fury convertible and hardtop coupe. They were the largest Plymouths ever, and naturally far roomier than the '64s. Unit construction continued, but a bolt-on subframe carried engine and front suspension. Powerplants ran from 225 slant six through 318, 361, 383, and wedgehead 426 V-8s with 230-365 bhp.

Meantime, the advent of intermediates, begun with Ford's 1962 Fairlane, suggested a new role for the 116-inch-wheelbase "standard" Plymouth of 1962-64. Duly re-skinned to resemble the big Fury, it was reborn for '65 as the mid-size Belvedere and met strong buyer approval. Offerings ran to Belvedere I sedans and wagon; Belvedere II four-door sedan, wagon, hardtop coupe, and convertible; bucket-seat, V-8-only Satellite hardtop and convertible; and a much-altered drag-oriented two-door aptly named Super Stock. A wedgehead 426 with 365/425 bhp was standard on S/S and optional for other Belvederes. S/S rode a special 115-inch chassis and weighed just 3170 pounds, so performance was mighty: 120 mph all out, 0-60 mph in eight seconds. But at $4671, it was neither cheap nor readily available. Normal Belvederes offered the same basic engines as were available in the Fury, but their base V-8 was a new small-block 273 rated at 180 bhp. This was actually a de-bored cousin of the 318, which was reengineered that year, becoming lighter, yet no less durable or potent.

Scoring points with performance-minded youngbloods, Plymouth finally took the incredible hemi from track to showroom as a limited-production option for the 1966 Belvedere II/Satellite. Heavy-duty suspension and oversize brakes were included to cope with the awesome power, ostensibly 425 bhp, but in reality, probably closer to 500. Initially, a four-speed manual was the only transmission offered, but three-speed TorqueFlite automatic was soon made available.

Surprisingly docile at low "touring" speeds, Hemi-Belvederes were electrifying demons when pushed. Correctly set up and with the proper tires and axle ratio, they could reach 120 mph in 12-13 seconds, making them prime quarter-mile competitors in the National Hot Rod Association's A/Stock and AA/Stock classes, along with Dodge's Coronet-based Hemi-Chargers. In addition, the mighty middleweights continued doing well in NASCAR: David Pearson won the '66 championship for Dodge; Richard Petty brought home the gold for Plymouth in '67.

With only detail changes, Belvedere/Satellite styling continued into 1967, the last year for the original '62 platform. Topping the line was the lush new Belvedere GTX, a hardtop coupe and convertible with a standard 375-bhp version of the big new 440 wedge (evolved from the 426) introduced on Chrysler's full-sized '66s. The '67 hemi option was exclusive to GTX, which was easily spotted: silver-and-black grille and back panel, simulated hood air intakes,

1961 Fury hardtop coupe

1961 Suburban Sport wagon

1962 Belvedere two-door sedan

1963 Belvedere hardtop coupe

1964 Sport Fury hardtop coupe

1966 VIP hardtop sedan

1965 Barracuda hardtop coupe

1966 Belvedere II hardtop coupe

1966 Barracuda hardtop coupe

1966 Valiant Signet hardtop coupe

sport striping, and dual exhausts.

A new body with no change in wheelbases gave Plymouth's 1968 intermediates a more rounded look that was just as pretty. Belvedere was reduced to a low-line coupe, sedan, and wagon; Satellite became the full-range volume series; Sport Satellite tagged a wagon, ragtop, and hardtop coupe priced just below GTX.

Plymouth scored a marketing coup for '68 with the Road Runner, a budget-priced, no-frills muscle machine with ingenious tie-ins to the beloved Warner Brothers cartoon character. It arrived as a pillared coupe, but unexpected popularity (2500 first-year sales forecast, almost 45,000 actual) prompted adding a two-door hardtop during the year. Exterior i.d. came from RR nameplates and cartoon-bird decals inside and out, along with side-facing dummy hood scoops that could be made functional for a little extra money. Power came from a 335-bhp 383 with 440 intake manifold and heads. The hemi was optional, as was a whole slew of comfort and cosmetic features, but beefy suspension, four-speed, and a cute "beep-beep" horn were standard. Dynamite on street or strip, this finely tuned package of power and performance cost only $2800-$3100.

Plymouth's mid-sized cars continued through 1970 with only minor changes. A convertible and more standard equipment bolstered the Road Runner's appeal for 1969, though higher prices didn't. The ragtop GTX disappeared after '69 and a mere 700 copies.

Following a mild '66 facelift, the big Furys received crisp new lower-body sheetmetal that added inches to length and width. Wheelbases and engines stayed largely the same, with the big-block 440 option returning from '66 with 350/375 bhp. Fury's standard V-8 remained a 230-bhp 318; a brace of optional 383s offered 270/325 bhp. The 225 slant six continued as the economy choice for all models.

Plymouth had joined Ford and Chevy in the move up to medium-price territory with the 1966 Fury VIP, a hardtop coupe and sedan with standard V-8, vinyl top, and a richly appointed interior. VIP returned as a separate series for '67 with the same two body styles, only the hardtop switched from notchback to "Fast Top" styling, with a slantback profile and very wide C-pillars that also showed up on a second Sport Fury hardtop. Pillarless Fury coupes offered the same choice of rooflines for 1968, when another mild facelift occurred.

If not exactly head-turners, the big late-Sixties Furys gave away nothing in appearance to rival Fords and Chevys. The 1965-66 models wore conservative full-width grilles, stacked quad headlamps, minimal side decoration, and simple taillights. Sheetmetal was more obviously sculptured for 1967-68, crisper yet somehow more imposing.

For 1969, the big Plymouths adopted the smoother, more massive "fuselage look" then favored by Chrysler stylists. Beltlines were higher, which made windows shorter, and lower-body contours more flowing but heavier-looking. Squarish fenderlines maintained a link with previous styling; headlamps reverted to horizontal pairs. Model offerings again stood pat, with non-wagon styles on an inch-longer wheelbase. Convertibles were waning fast by this time. The '69 Fury III ragtop saw only 4129 copies; the Sport Fury a mere 1579. The latter disappeared entirely for 1970, leaving the bench-seat job as Plymouth's last big ragtop.

Valiant was the product that sustained Plymouth during its early-Sixties troubles. One of the Big Three's original 1960 compacts, it was ostensibly a separate make that first year, then always wore Plymouth badges. The debut design ran through 1962: ruggedly built "Unibody" cars with Exner styling marked by square grilles, pronounced "blade" fenderlines, and short decks adorned by dummy spare tires, all on a 106-inch wheelbase. A four-door sedan and wagon were initially offered in V100 and V200 trim. A V100 two-door sedan and V200 hardtop coupe arrived for 1961. With bucket seats and spiffy trim, the latter became the 1962 Signet 200, perhaps the most collectible early Valiant.

One of Valiant's strong points was its robust slant six, canted to the right to permit lower hoodlines, though engineers also claimed certain manufacturing and operational benefits. The initial 170-cid version produced 101 bhp; a 1960-61 four-barrel option called "Hyper-Pack" raised that to 148 bhp. The larger 225 unit from the big Plymouths became optional from 1962.

Exner's departure left Elwood Engel to shape the '63

Valiant, which was clean, if a bit stodgy. Bolstered by appealing new Signet and V200 convertibles, Valiant picked up sales; the '64s picked up even more with optional availability of the new 273 small-block V-8, which made these cars sprightly indeed. After two facelift years, Valiant was completely redesigned for 1967, adopting a 108-inch wheelbase and four-square lines reminiscent of some midsize European sedans. Wagons, curiously enough, were dropped, yet Valiant remained Detroit's top-selling compact.

The success of Chevy's Corvair Monza prompted Plymouth to refocus its sights on the sporty-compact market. The result was the Barracuda, launched in mid-1964 as a '65 model. This was not a reply to Ford's Mustang "ponycar," though some observers thought otherwise, as the cars appeared almost simultaneously. Actually, Barracuda was little more than a Valiant with a new superstructure: a fastback hardtop coupe with a huge compound-curve backlight. This made for a stubby trunklid, but a fold-down back seat (then a novelty for Detroit) could be used to create a seven-foot-long cargo deck for hauling things like surfboards and hero sandwiches. Despite its obvious workaday origins, Barracuda offered a pleasing combination of

1966 VIP hardtop coupe

1967 Barracuda hardtop coupe

1967 Sport Fury fastback hardtop coupe

1968 Barracuda convertible coupe

1968 Sport Satellite convertible coupe

1968 Sport Fury fastback hardtop coupe

1969 Road Runner convertible coupe

1969 Sport Fury convertible coupe

1969 Sport Fury hardtop coupe

1969 Barracuda fastback hardtop coupe

sporty looks, good handling, utility, and room for four. Nearly 65,000 were sold in its first full model year—far below Mustang volume, but welcome added business.

Predictably, the 225 slant six was standard for the 1964-65 Barracuda, with the 180-bhp 273 V-8 optional. However, a high-performance 235-bhp 273 was also offered, sporting high-lift/high-overlap camshaft, domed pistons, solid lifters, dual-contact breaker points, unsilenced air cleaner, and a sweet-sounding, low-restriction exhaust system. With Rallye Suspension (heavy-duty front torsion bars and anti-sway bars, stiff rear leaf springs), Firm-Ride shocks, and a four-speed gearbox, the 235-bhp job could do 0-60 mph in eight seconds flat and the standing quarter-mile in 16 seconds.

After a debatable '66 facelift dominated by a two-piece eggcrate grille, Barracuda was handsomely redesigned for '67. Wheelbase was stretched by two inches, overall length by five inches, and a shapelier fastback was joined by a new convertible and notchback hardtop coupe (with rather oddly kinked rear roofline). A newly available V-8, a four-barrel 383 with 280 bhp, provided better straightline performance, but hurt handling by adding up to 300 extra pounds up front. The 273 remained a better choice. As for '66, a Formula S package was offered comprising heavy-duty suspension, tachometer, wide-oval tires, and special stripes and badges.

Happily, this Barracuda continued without drastic change through 1969. A vertical-bar grille insert marked the '68s; a checked insert and revamped taillights the '69s. In both years there were muscle-market "Cuda" models marketed with a new 340 small-block (a bored-out 318) packing 275 bhp, or a big-block 383 with 300 bhp for '68 and 330 bhp for '69.

Like buyers then, collectors now flock to the most exciting Plymouths—anything with a hemi as well as the mid-size Road Runners and GTXs. However, Plymouth convertibles, Valiant to Fury, are still reasonably priced yet often rare (only 1516 of the '62 Sport Furys, for example); they're probably among the last undiscovered treasures of this decade. The best choice for "one-car" collectors is a Barracuda, particularly a 1967-69. Clean, lithe, and much better built than earlier Plymouths, it could be an outstanding road car in Formula S form, at least enough for most enthusiasts. And unlike Mustang, it didn't "cannibalize" sales from other models in its maker's line—something Plymouth probably wishes it could say today.

PLYMOUTH AT A GLANCE, 1960-1969									
	1960	1961	1962	1963	1964	1965	1966	1967	1968	1969
Price Range, $	2053-3134	1955-3136	1930-3082	1910-3082	1921-3095	2004-4671	2025-3251	2117-3418	2254-3543	2094-3718
Weight Range, lbs.	2635-4020	2565-3995	2480-3455	2515-3590	2540-3630	2560-4200	2600-4175	2645-4135	2655-4100	2656-4173
Wheelbases, in.	106.5-122	106.5-122	106.5-116	106-116	106-116	106-121	106-121	108-122	108-122	108-122
6 Cyl. Engines, hp	101-148	101-148	101-145	101-145	101-145	101-145	101-145	115-145	115-145	115-145
8 Cyl. Engines, hp	230-330	230-375	230-420	230-425	180-425	180-425	180-425	180-425	190-425	190-425

PONTIAC

Pontiac was Detroit's biggest success story of the Sixties—a distinction it was destined to repeat in the 1980s. The reason was the same in both decades: enthusiast-oriented chief executives (Semon E. "Bunkie" Knudsen and William C. Hoglund, respectively) who made Pontiac synonymous with high performance.

Much of the division's Sixties surge can be credited to the compact Tempest and its later mid-size evolutions. The debut '61 was significant for having GM's first postwar four-cylinder engine, an innovative flexible driveshaft, four-wheel independent suspension, and a rear transaxle (a transmission in unit with the differential).

One buff magazine said the Tempest "sets many new trends and unquestionably is a prototype of the American car for the Sixties." But no U.S. producer ever copied its radical driveline (though Porsche would use something similar later on) and Detroit wouldn't shift strongly to fours until the early Eighties. The 1961-63 Tempests were fairly popular, but their orthodox successors sold far bet-

ter. The original powerplant, a 195-cubic-inch unit with 110/130 horsepower (basically half of Pontiac's 389 V-8), was abandoned on the '64s for an inline six.

Like a speedometer cable, the '61 Tempest's so-called "rope" driveshaft carried rotary motion through a gentle curve—a long bar that bent slightly beneath the floor, thin but lightly stressed. Carried within a steel tube, it mounted on bearings and was permanently lubricated. Its slight sag reduced floor-hump height in front, though not in back. In addition, the design eliminated the need for universal joints and allowed softer engine mounts for better noise isolation. A first for Detroit, if not the world, the rear transaxle made Tempest less nose-heavy than its conventional cousins, the Olds F-85 and Buick Special. But though the independent rear suspension was ostensibly superior, it made the car prone to sudden oversteer that could be alarming on wet roads. Still, the Tempest generally handled well, more orthodox than Chevy's aft-engine Corvair with its even trickier rear swing axles.

1960 Catalina convertible coupe

1961 Ventura Sport hardtop coupe

1961 Bonneville Sport hardtop coupe

1962 Grand Prix Sport hardtop coupe

1962 Tempest LeMans convertible coupe

The initial 112-inch-wheelbase Tempest shared its basic Y-body unitized structure with the compact F-85 and Special. Its standard four teamed with both manual and automatic transaxles, and was offered in several stages of tune to suit regular or premium gas. By 1963, horsepower was up to 115-166. Optionally available for 1961-62 was the aluminum 215-cid Buick V-8 with 155/185 bhp. This was replaced for '63 by a debored 326-cid version of the Pontiac 389 packing 260 bhp. So equipped, the Tempest was quick: able to scale 0-60 mph in 9.5 seconds and reach 115 mph.

Tempest arrived in a single series with standard- and Custom-trim four-door sedans and four-door Safari wagon with one-piece rear "liftgate." A pillared coupe bowed at mid-season with a choice of bench- or sportier

bucket-seat interiors, the latter christened LeMans. Deluxe and LeMans convertibles were added for '62 and proved quite popular, prompting a separate LeMans series for '63. Styling didn't change much in these years. A twin-oval grille was used for '61, a full-width three-section affair for '62, a revived split grille and squarer body lines for '63. Prices didn't change much either, with most models in $2200-$2500 territory.

For 1964, GM lengthened its compacts to a 115-inch wheelbase—which made them intermediates. A redesigned Tempest bearing taut, geometric lines was issued on this corporate A-body platform shared with Chevrolet's new Chevelle, the Olds F-85/Cutlass, and Buick's Special/Skylark. But the real excitement came with the mid-season

1963 Grand Prix Sport hardtop coupe

1963 Tempest LeMans convertible coupe

1964 Bonneville convertible coupe

1964 Catalina Sport hardtop coupe

1963 Bonneville Sport hardtop coupe

1964 Tempest GTO sport coupe

1965 Tempest Lemans GTO convertible coupe

1965 Catalina 2 + 2 convertible coupe

debut of the Tempest GTO, the first of the "muscle cars." The nickname was well taken. With the right options, a GTO could deliver unprecedented performance.

Most GTOs had to be "built" from the sales catalog. For 1964 you started with a Tempest coupe, hardtop coupe, or convertible, then checked off the GTO package on the order form: floorshift, 389 V-8, quick steering, stiff shocks, dual exhaust, and premium tires, all for about $300. From there you were on your own: four-speed gearbox ($188); metallic brake linings, heavy-duty radiator, and limited-slip differential ($75 for the lot); 348-bhp 389 ($115). At that point, all you needed was a lead foot—and lots of gas.

Sports-car purists took umbrage at Pontiac's use of GTO (*gran turismo omologato*, an Italian term meaning approved production-based racing car), but an outspoken enthusiast magazine bravely answered the critics by comparing Pontiac's GTO with Ferrari's. A good Pontiac, they said, would trim the Ferrari in a drag race and lose on a road course. But "with the addition of NASCAR road racing suspension, the Pontiac will take the measure of any Ferrari other than prototype racing cars.... The Ferrari costs $20,000. With every conceivable option on a GTO, it would be difficult to spend more than $3800. That's a bargain."

The successful LeMans/Tempest formula saw relatively little change through 1967. Vertical headlights and crisper styling arrived for '65. The '66s had three-inch-longer bodies with smoother contours, including arched, "Coke-bottle" rear fenders.

For 1968 came a new GM A-body with dual wheelbases—116 inches on four-doors, 112 on two-doors—plus revamped styling that continued to display big-Pontiac elements such as a large bumper/grille and, on hardtop coupes, more rakish fastback rooflines. Standard for GTO was a new 400-cid extension of the 389 pumping out 350 bhp; 360 bhp was optional via "Ram-Air," a functional hood scoop. The '68 GTO also featured a neatly integrated energy-absorbing front bumper covered in color-keyed Endura plastic.

The mid-size Pontiacs would continue in this basic form through 1972. Collectors have since tended to prefer the tidier pre-1971 models. Among the mildly facelifted '69s was a hotter GTO: "The Judge," with colorful striping, a 366-bhp Ram-Air 400, and three-speed manual gearbox with Hurst shifter.

The base engine on 1964-65 Tempests was a 215-cid inline six from Oldsmobile rated at 140 bhp. For 1966 came a surprise replacement: a European-style overhead-cam six. Sized at 230 cid, it developed 165 bhp standard or 207 bhp in "Sprint" form (via Rochester Quadra-Jet carburetor, wilder timing, and double valve springs). Crankshafts had seven main bearings; the single camshaft was driven by a fiberglass-reinforced notched belt rather than conventional chain or gear drive.

So equipped, the '66 Tempest was a satisfying performer, if hardly in the GTO's league. The typical Sprint could do 0-60 mph in 10 seconds and reach 115 mph. With options like bucket seats, console and four-speed floorshift, the clean-lined Sprint had the look and feel of a true grand touring car. A longer stroke took the ohc engine to 250 cid for 1968, good for 175 bhp or, as a Sprint, 215 bhp (230 bhp

1966 2 + 2 convertible coupe

1966 Catalina hardtop coupe

1966 Tempest GTO hardtop coupe

1967 Tempest GTO hardtop coupe

1967 Grand Prix convertible coupe

1967 Firebird hardtop coupe

1967 Catalina convertible coupe

1968 Firebird hardtop coupe

1968 Grand Prix hardtop coupe

for '69). Sadly, it proved less than reliable and, like the Tempest four before it, departed after 1969 in favor of a conventional overhead-valve Chevy six of the same size.

With Pontiac's performance image secure by the mid-Sixties, division managers knew that their Firebird "ponycar" had to be something special—especially since it would use the basic 108-inch-wheelbase F-body structure of Chevrolet's new-for-'67 Camaro. But the Firebird *was* different, sporting a divided grille of the sort now expected of Pontiacs and offering an optional 400 with 325 bhp. The base-tune ohc six was initially standard; the optional Sprint version made for a sprightly yet economical performer.

Debuting about six months behind Camaro, the Firebird wasn't modified much through early 1970. A change of engines made the '67 Firebird 326 a 350 model for '68, when side marker lights were added per federal decree. The '69s were restyled below the belt and gained a host of government-ordered safety features. Convertibles continued until "1970½," when the all-new coupe-only second generation arrived.

Of course, the hottest and most memorable early Firebird was the '69 Trans Am, a $725 option package announced in March and loosely inspired by the Firebirds that were half-heartedly contesting the Trans-American road-racing series. Special badges, a decklid spoiler, and white paint with twin dorsal racing stripes identified it. A 335-bhp Ram Air III 400 gave it great go, while a heavily fortified chassis and brakes made for superb roadability. Only 697 of the '69s were built, including a mere eight convertibles. A slight 55 cars were equipped with the optional 345-bhp Ram Air IV engine. Happily, the T/A was destined for much greater success, and would earn it soon enough.

Though sometimes overlooked in the excitement surrounding its smaller models, Pontiac built some of Detroit's best-looking, best-handling standard cars of the Sixties—and the public loved them. Sales jumped from about 400,000 for 1960 to nearly half a million by '69. On a divisional basis, Pontiac ran third to Chevrolet and Ford from 1962 all the way to 1970, and these big cars had a lot to do with it.

They began the decade as facelifted versions of the highly successful "Wide Track" '59s, bearing high "twin-tube" taillamps and a vee'd, full-width, horizontal-bar grille. A fourth series was added, the Catalina-based Ventura, with a hardtop coupe and Vista hardtop sedan priced just below Star Chief. Both were dropped for '62 in favor of the bucket-seat Grand Prix, an elegantly tailored hardtop coupe, also on the low-line Catalina chassis. A fast-riser on the sales charts, the GP finished the decade outdrawing all other full-size Pontiacs save for Catalinas—and with just a single body style. Well, almost. A GP convertible, offered only for 1967, is now a minor collector's item.

Big-Pontiac styling kept improving, at least through '66. The distinctive split grille returned for 1961, along with crisp new Bill Mitchell lines on shorter wheelbases: 119 inches for Catalina/Ventura, 123 on Star Chief and Bonneville, 119 inches for wagons. Catalina added an inch for '62. Clean machines with stacked quad headlamps and narrow, split grilles appeared for 1963-64. The '65s were well executed, but had a massive, bulging front and billowy bodysides, both deemphasized for '66. Wheelbase lengthened to 121 inches for Catalina/GP/wagons and to 124 inches for Star Chief/Bonneville.

Alas, the '67s looked even bulkier, with heavy, curved rear fenders. For 1968 came a huge bumper/grille with prominent vertical center bulge. Both wheelbases tacked on another inch for '69, when the schnoz was toned down.

Pontiac's full-size line was remarkably consistent in the Sixties. Catalinas were offered in all the usual body styles throughout, along with a mid-range Star Chief sedan and hardtop sedan. The latter plus a hardtop coupe, big convertible, and Safari comprised the top-line Bonneville series. A bucket-seat Catalina "2+2" arrived for 1964 as an extra-cost package for the convertible and two-door hardtop. It became a distinct series for '66, then vanished in the fast-fading market for sporty full-sizers. The only change involved Star Chief. It tacked on the name Executive for '66, which then supplanted Star Chief through 1970.

Engines powering the big Pontiacs were also quite consistent in the Sixties, with numerous horsepower variations in just four basic sizes—two large and two "small"—all derived from the division's original 1955 V-8. The juniors were a 389 through 1966 and a bored-out 400 from '67. Standard for all models, they ranged from 215 to 350 bhp, with the latter also powering 1967-70 Grand Prixs. The senior units, optional on most models, were a 421 for 1963-66 and a 428 through '69, after which a 455 took over. Horsepower peaked at 376 for '67, then began declining with federally mandated emission controls. A monster 427-bhp 421 powered a lightweight 1963-64 Catalina drag-racing special featuring aluminum body panels, plastic side windows, and a drilled-out frame.

Though Pontiac never reached the "one horsepower per cubic inch" ideal like Chevy and Olds, its big-block V-8s were more than enough, most big "Ponchos" being quite fast. They were also surprisingly roadable with their "Wide-Track" stance and taut suspensions—certainly more so than most other big cars of the Sixties.

Luxury, performance, comfort, and handling in full-size cars, consistent innovation, solid value, and, occasionally, exhilarating speed in compacts and intermediates—no wonder Pontiac was so successful in the Sixties.

1968 Tempest GTO hardtop coupe

1969 Firebird Trans Am convertible coupe

1968 Grand Prix hardtop coupe

1969 Tempest GTO "The Judge" hardtop coupe

PONTIAC AT A GLANCE, 1960-1969									
	1960	1961	1962	1963	1964	1965	1966	1967	1968	1969
Price Range, $	2631-3530	2113-3530	2186-3624	2188-3623	2259-3633	2260-3632	2278-3747	2341-3819	2461-3987	2510-4104
Weight Range, lbs.	3835-4360	2785-4185	2785-4255	2810-4245	2930-4275	2930-4310	3040-4390	2955-4415	3061-4485	3080-4600
Wheelbases, in.	122-124	112-123	112-123	112-123	115-123	115-124	115-124	108-124	108-124	108-125
4 Cyl. Engines, hp		110-130	110-115	115-166						
6 Cyl. Engines, hp					140	140	165-207	165-215	175-215	175-230
8 Cyl. Engines, hp	215-348	155-373	185-405	215-410	230-370	250-376	250-376	250-376	265-390	265-390

Rambler entered the Sixties a strong player, only to vanish as a name at decade's end. America's pioneer compact gained enough ground by the late Fifties to challenge Plymouth for the industry's number three position. It then staked that claim for 1961. Its cars were perfect for the prevailing market—and that was the problem. The market changed radically within a few years, partly due to Rambler's success, prompting American Motors to move from sensible economy to bigger, brighter, brawnier cars in an attempt to match the Big Three on every front.

For a time, things remained rosy. After more than 422,000 cars for 1960, Rambler recorded its unprecedented third-place finish despite '61 volume that was actually down some 12 percent. Output recovered to a bit over 423,000 for '62, though Rambler could claim only fifth as Pontiac and Oldsmobile swept by. Then the decade peak: a smashing 428,000-plus for 1963. It was the highest volume an independent would ever record, but was good for only eighth place. Two years later, Rambler/AMC had dropped to ninth; by 1968 it stood 10th.

Two managerial changes greatly affected Rambler in this period. Hard-driving George Romney, AMC's first president, left in 1962 to become governor of Michigan. His successor, Roy Abernethy, began the product diversification that would ultimately prove misguided; he also began deemphasizing the Rambler name. Abernethy stepped aside in 1966 for Roy D. Chapin, Jr., who became board chairman the following year, with William V. Luneberg taking over as president. This team ordered further diversification, including new "make models" like Javelin, and killed off Rambler after 1969. As a marque, it had simply outlived its usefulness.

The foundation of AMC's early success, the 108-inch-wheelbase unit-body Rambler of 1956, was first sold by both Nash and Hudson, which had merged to form AMC two years before. Rambler as a distinct marque appeared for 1957, when the last Nashes and Hudsons were built, but the car itself changed little aside from a new V-8 option. It was then heavily reworked, acquiring bulkier, more squarish outer sheetmetal and little tailfins for 1958-59. Models comprised pillared and pillarless sedans and wagons in Six and Rebel V-8 series, as well as a similar line of new, upmarket Rambler Ambassadors with 327 V-8 power and a 117-inch wheelbase (achieved solely by a lengthened front end), replacing Nash/Hudson as AMC's senior cars.

Another major restyle brought smoother lines, full-width grilles, and less-intrusive sloped-back A-pillars (replacing vertical) for 1960. The 108-inch-wheelbase line was retagged Rambler Classic for '61, when a lower hood and eggcrate grille appeared. The '62s gained a more involved face and lost the vestigial fins. An interesting '62 option was "E-Stick," a manual transmission with "automatic" clutch. Though it cost but $60, it was too complex to promote much interest.

Richard A. Teague had joined the AMC styling staff by then, but it was departing designer Edmund A. Anderson who crafted the handsome '63 Ramblers that won *Motor Trend* magazine's "Car of the Year" Award. Featured were a wholly new 112-inch-wheelbase unibody platform with a lower silhouette and smoothly rounded bodysides empha-

sized by curved door glass, plus one-piece door-frame structures—a Detroit first. Though the Classic was still a bit chunky, it looked nicer than ever.

Teague refined this design once Anderson left, giving '64 Classics a flat grille (replacing concave) and stainless-steel rocker moldings. Hardtops returned after a year's absence, but only as two-doors. Continued from '63 were two- and four-door sedans and pillared four-door Cross Country wagons in 550, 660, and 770 series (respectively replacing

1960 Ambassador Custom hardtop wagon

1960 American four-door sedan

1960 American two-door wagon

1961 Ambassador Custom four-door sedan

the former Deluxe, Super, and Custom). There were two hardtops: bench-seat 770 and a limited-edition bucket-seater called Typhoon.

Classic added a convertible for '65, when grilles became convex "dumbbell" affairs, hoods got recontoured, and rear decks were lengthened and squared-up. The ragtop appeared only in the 770 line, where Typhoon reappeared as the 770H. Styling was the same for '66 save grilles, minor trim, a new "crisp line" hardtop roof, and a reworked wagon rear end. The 770H was renamed Rebel.

Also new for '65 was a hastily conjured Classic offshoot, the bucket-seat Marlin fastback. Intended to battle the Ford Mustang and Plymouth Barracuda, it wore a sweeping pillarless roof that tapered down and inward at the rear. Teague penned elliptical rear side windows to keep things light-looking, but the Classic's relatively stubby hood made for ungainly overall proportions. This likely explains why the new image-maker didn't sell too well despite decent performance and a reasonable $3100 base price. Only 10,327 were produced for '65, after which Marlin was sold as its own "make" for another two years, though with diminishing success (see AMC).

Rebel replaced Classic entirely on an all-new group of mid-size '67 Ramblers. Besides a roomier new body/chassis on a two-inch longer wheelbase (114 inches), there was handsome, contemporary Teague styling with a "floating" rectangular grille, squarish front fenders that flowed back into "hippy" rear fenders, and a shapely deck with large, canted taillights. The lineup was reduced to two sedans and one wagon in 550 trim; mid-range 770 sedan, wagon, and hardtop; and sporty SST convertible and hardtop. Rebel then became a separate make, too (see AMC).

Mid-size Ramblers entered the Sixties with two basic engines: six and V-8. The former, a holdover from Nash days, was a long-stroke 195.6-cubic-incher that made 127/138 horsepower as the standard Six/Classic engine through 1965. A lighter new short-stroke 232 "Torque Command" unit with 145 bhp began replacing it for '64, and spawned a destroked 128-bhp 199 as standard for '64 Classic 550s. The 232 initially featured in the '64 Typhoon hardtop (of which 2500 were built, all yellow with black vinyl roof covering), would become standard for Classic/Rebel beginning in 1966. An optional 155-bhp alternative was listed for 1965-67.

The V-8, designed by AMC for late Nash/Hudson applications, continued in mid-size Ramblers through 1961 as a 250 with 200/215 bhp. A bored-out 287 derivative with 198 bhp replaced it for '63. V-8 Classics offered performance with economy. Even with optional "Flash-O-Matic" self-shift transmission (bought from Borg-Warner) they could do 0-60 mph in about 10 seconds and return 16-20 miles per gallon. But the V-8s were heavier than the sixes, so understeer was pronounced since the front wheels carried no less than 57 percent of total vehicle weight.

For '67 Rebels, the 287 V-8 was stroked to 290 cid for 200 optional horses. This replaced the Ambassador "big-block" 327 with 250/270 bhp that had been a mid-size option since '65. Also new for '67 was a 290 bored out to 343 cid, which provided 235-280 bhp depending on tune.

AMC's smallest Sixties car was the American, which

1961 Classic Custom Cross Country four-door wagon

1961 Ambassador Custom Cross Country four-door wagon

1962 American two-door sedan

1962 Ambassador four-door sedan

1963 American 440 convertible coupe

1963 Ambassador 990 two-door sedan

1963 Ambassador 990 Cross Country four-door wagon

1964 American 440 convertible coupe

1964 Ambassador 990H hardtop coupe

1965 American 440 convertible coupe

through 1963 harked back to the original Pininfarina-designed 1950 Rambler. That 100-inch-wheelbase compact had been dropped for '56, but was revived to excellent sales effect in the economy-car boom of 1958. Little changed through 1960, though by that time the American was an anachronism with its dated styling and ancient 90-bhp, 195.6-cid Nash L-head six. Deluxe, Super, and Custom sedans and wagons were offered from $1781. Attractive prices combined with economical simplicity for healthy sales—enough to justify a full restyle for 1961.

Alas, it was another odd Ed Anderson effort: boxy and truncated, three-inches narrower and 5.2-inches shorter overall. Happily, the old six was updated with an overhead-valve cylinder head (actually a mid-1960 development), which lifted optional bhp to 127, though base output remained at 90. The lineup sprinkled two- and four-door sedans and wagons plus a new convertible among the usual trim variations. Posh "400" models were added for '62. Series were retitled for '63—low-end 220, mid-priced 330, and top-end 440—and hardtop coupes arrived: a bench-seat 440 and bucket-seat 440H. Though true economy cars with fair interior room, the 1961-63 Americans were hardly beautiful.

Fortunately, Teague was able to change that for '64. The result was a pretty and clever adaptation of the '63 Classic, its structure shortened ahead of the cowl from a 112- to a 106-inch wheelbase. That was still half a foot longer than American's previous span, and Teague used it well, producing a clean, shapely compact with curved side glass and only modest brightwork—quite apropos for its market. This styling would prove so good that the '64 American could carry on to decade's end with only minor changes.

The '64 American line repeated 1963's, only to thin for '66, when the 440H became a Rogue. A ragtop Rogue was new for '67, then vanished for '68, when the roster was cut to Rogue hardtop, two base-trim sedans, and 440 four-door sedan and wagon. Sixes continued to dominate American sales, with new-generation 199- and 232-cid engines delivering 128/145 horsepower from 1967. But 1966 brought American's first V-8 options, the new 290 in 200- and 225-bhp tune. Both continued through Rambler's last stand for '69, when American prices still began just shy of the magic $2000 mark.

Perhaps as an outrageous farewell to the Rambler name, AMC issued the SC/Rambler for 1969, a limited-edition Rogue with a big 315-bhp 390 V-8, functional hood scoop, Hurst four-speed, heavy-duty chassis, and loud red, white, and blue color scheme. Priced at $2998, the "Scrambler," as it was inevitably nicknamed, was hardly in the sensible Rambler tradition. Road tests confirmed AMC's claim of standing quarter-miles in the low 14s at around 100 mph. Production ended at 1512 units, though that was triple the planned run.

Ambassador remained AMC's "standard" or "full-size" car in the Sixties, though it also remained mostly an elongated Rambler with nicer furnishings—which is probably why sales were never high. AMC even let buyers in on the game by applying Rambler nameplates through 1965, after which Ambassador joined Marlin as a separate make.

The first non-Nash Ambassador had been planned as the

1958 Nash and Hudson, but became a Rambler when AMC gave up on those names. Like their 108-inch-wheelbase linemates, the 1960-61 models were restyled continuations of the blocky 1958-59 design, still somewhat ornate inside and overdecorated outside. The '61s were notable for their distinctly ugly sloped front. Prices spanned the $2400-$3200 range, with the cheapest offering a Deluxe pillared four-door sedan. Also on hand were Super and Custom wagons with six or eight seats, and Super and Custom sedans. Like Classic, the '62 line added extra-luxurious "400" models with higher-quality trim and standard automatic, but moved down to the intermediate's 108-inch wheelbase. Ambassador's only engine through 1964 was a 327 V-8 with 250 bhp standard or 270 bhp with optional four-barrel carburetor.

The new '63 Classic implied a new Ambassador as well. Styling differences were minimal save the usual extra chrome on Ambassadors. Pillarless styles departed, and series were retitled 800, 880, and 990, each with a pair of sedans and wagons. The 800s were tough to sell and vanished for '64. So did the 990s, leaving just a four-door sedan and wagon, plus a new hardtop coupe. The last was also offered as a sporty bucket-seat 990H with standard 270-bhp V-8.

The '64 line sold no better than the '63, so for 1965 the Ambassador was restored to its own, longer (116-inch) wheelbase. Also back was a two-series 880/990 lineup (including 990H), but standard power was now a 155-bhp 232 six. The base V-8 was the new small-block 287, with optional 327s as before. An outer-sheetmetal redo bestowed linear lines à la Classic, with distinction in a "bi-level" grille flanked by stacked quad headlights. Ambassador also followed Classic for '65 by offering its first convertible, a 990. Trunk space improved on all models but passenger room didn't, mainly because the restored extra wheelbase again occurred ahead of the cowl. There were almost no changes for '66, save Ambassador being marketed as a separate make.

AMC didn't build that many convertibles in the Sixties, no surprise given its much smaller volume against the Big Three. The American ragtop ran a full seven years (1961-67), but the open Classic/Rebel lasted only four years (1965-68); the counterpart Ambassador just three (1965-67). AMC's busiest soft-top season was 1965, when it built 3882 Americans, 4953 Classics, and 3499 Ambassadors. All AMC convertibles stand to grow in both collector esteem and dollar value as the years continue to roll by.

1965 Marlin hardtop coupe

1967 Rebel SST hardtop coupe

1968 Rogue hardtop coupe

1969 Hurst SC/Rambler hardtop coupe

RAMBLER AT A GLANCE, 1960-1969										
	1960	1961	1962	1963	1964	1965	1966	1967	1968	1969
Price Range, $	1781-3151	1833-3113	1832-3023	1832-3018	1907-2985	1979-3100	2017-2629	2073-2872	1946-2426	1998-2998
Weight Range, lbs.	2428-3592	2454-3566	2454-3471	2446-3305	2506-3350	2490-3268	2554-3071	2591-3288	2604-2800	2604-3160
Wheelbases, in.	100-117	100-117	100-108	100-112	106-112	106-116	106-112	106-114	106	106
6 Cyl. Engines, hp	90-138	90-138	90-138	90-138	90-145	90-155	128-155	128-155	128-145	128-145
8 Cyl. Engines, hp	200-270	200-270	250-270	198-270	198-270	198-270	198-270	200-280	200-225	200-315

SHELBY

Carroll Shelby retired as a race driver in 1960, going on to become America's most charismatic force in high-performance specialty cars. Beginning in 1962, he built or contributed to several blindingly fast, raceworthy machines, all "Powered by Ford": the stark Anglo-American Shelby-Cobra 289 and 427 roadsters, the happy little Sunbeam Tiger two-seater, and the mid-engine Ford GT40 and Mark IV prototypes. The last took Dearborn to its racing pinnacle by winning the gruelling 24 Hours of LeMans in 1966-67.

Shelby's best-known Sixties project was the limited-edition Mustang GT. The first, named GT-350 for no particular reason, was a super-tuned version of Ford's new 1965-66 "ponycar," a conversion carried out by Carroll's small Shelby-American operation in Los Angeles. Early GT-350s were uncompromisingly potent grand touring cars that were equally at home on the track. Post-1967 Shelbys were planned and built by Ford, and were thus not quite as hairy, though they were still plenty exciting.

The GT-350 was created mainly to win the Sports Car Club of America's national B-production championship—which it did hands down—in 1965-67, thus giving showroom Mustangs a "competition-proved" aura. Each one began as a white Mustang fastback with blue racing stripes powered by the high-performance version of Ford's excellent 289-cubic-inch small-block V-8. Shelby added high-rise manifold, bigger four-barrel carburetor, and free-flow exhaust headers, which with other changes brought horsepower from 271 to 306 at 6000 rpm. All early GT-350s carried the Borg-Warner T-10 four-speed gearbox (a regular Mustang option) and a stronger rear axle from the full-size Ford Galaxie in place of the stock Mustang's Falcon unit.

Other notable component features included Koni shock absorbers, Shelby-cast 15-inch alloy wheels shod with

1965 Shelby GT 350 fastback coupe

high-performance Goodyear tires, metallic shoes/pads for the rear-drum/front-disc brakes, and fast-ratio steering (via relocated front suspension mounting points). A hefty steel tube was installed linking the tops of the front shock towers in order to minimize body flex in hard cornering. The result of all this was nearly neutral handling, versus Mustang's strong understeer.

Outside, a fiberglass hood with prominent, functional scoop and competition-style tiedowns replaced the stock Mustang item. Shelby also removed the prancing horse from the grille, and opened up the fake bodyside scoops for rear-brake cooling. For '66, the fastback's rear-roof air-extractor grilles were replaced with plastic quarter windows. Interior changes began with three-inch competition seatbelts, mahogany-rimmed steering wheel, and steering-column-mounted tachometer. To meet racing rules for "sport cars" (defined as two-seaters), the rear seat was removed and the spare tire lashed down in its place. For '66, however, Shelby offered a kit that restored the back bench and returned the spare to the trunk.

As planned, Shelby also developed a competition GT-350R powered by the same basic engine as racing 289 Cobras. That meant a nominal 350 bhp—an astounding

1967 GT 500 fastback coupe

1968 GT 500 fastback coupe

1.21 bhp per cubic inch. To minimize weight, the gearbox got an aluminum case, the interior was stripped, and a racing seat was installed along with a roll bar and safety harness. Competition tires and super-duty suspension were specified, and a special fiberglass nose eliminated the front bumper while providing a rudimentary air dam with a central slot for extra airflow to the engine. A few GT-350Rs were built with all-disc brakes, a 400-bhp engine, and wide tires under flared fenders.

Hertz Rent-A-Car got into the act in 1966 by ordering 936 special GT-350H models. All carried Ford's three-speed self-shift Cruise-O-Matic and black paint set off by gold stripes. Hertz rented them for $17 a day and 17 cents a mile. Weekend racers were naturally among the renters, and their unauthorized track use quickly made the venture unprofitable, leading Hertz to abandon it after one year.

In all, Shelby built 562 GT-350s for '65 and another 2380 to '66 specs, including R-model racers and the Hertz units, plus six prototype '66 convertibles. That was good for such a specialized machine, but cost-conscious Ford wanted even higher volume. As a result, the original Shelby concept started to be watered down.

1968 GT 350 convertible coupe

1969 GT 500 fastback coupe

Ford bowed a heavier, restyled 1967 Mustang with a first-time 390 big-block option. Carroll predictably went Ford one better by tossing in the firm's even bigger new 428 engine to create a companion model, the GT-500. Horsepower was advertised at 335, mainly so insurance companies wouldn't worry, but true output was closer to 400. The GT-350 returned with its previous power rating, but the figure was now really below 300, because the previous steel-tube exhaust headers had been eliminated in deference to noise regulations.

Both '67 Shelbys wore a longer and more aggressive new fiberglass front end, crisply clipped "Kamm" tail with prominent spoiler, and other appearance departures from regular Mustangs, plus small chassis refinements. Interiors featured a large black-painted roll bar with new inertia-reel seatbelts built in. Shelby built 3225 of the '67 GTs, which sold for around $4000, down some $500 from the 1965-66 cars that were themselves incredible high-performance buys.

The 350 and 500 returned for '68, but were somewhat less special. Interiors, for instance, were stock Mustang save a console-mounted ammeter and oil-pressure gauge, while luxury options like air conditioning and power steering proliferated. Styling was modified with a wider hood scoop and big Mercury Cougar taillights with sequential turn signals. Convertibles arrived at about $100 higher than comparable fastbacks. At mid-season, GT-500s became GT-500KRs ("King of the Road"), the name denoting substitution of Ford's 428 "Cobra Jet" engine with extra-large ports and a new intake manifold fed by a huge 735-cfm four-barrel Holley carb. Fastback prices rose to $4117 for the 350, $4317 for the 500 and $4473 for the KR. The costliest '68 Shelby was the KR convertible at $4594.

With Ford now calling all the shots, the '69 Shelbys be-came even more like showroom Mustangs, which were fully redesigned that year. Styling was still distinctive but busier, with a loop bumper/grille, scoops and ducts most everywhere, and reflective tape stripes midway up the flanks. GT-350s were demoted to Ford's new 351 Cleveland V-8 with 290 bhp; GT-500s stayed with the Cobra Jet engine, still at a nominal 335 bhp, but were no longer KRs.

Suddenly, it was all over. After just 3150 cars for '69, plus 636 leftovers reserialized as 1970s, Shelby and Ford president Lee Iacocca agreed to cancel the GT program. Tightening government regulations, spiraling insurance rates (the cars' accident record was staggering) and interference from hot new Mustangs like Mach 1 and Boss 302 had done them in, but they were the ultimate ponycars. Today, they're among the ultimate in collector cars.

Circumstances would again team Shelby and Iacocca at Chrysler about a dozen years hence. By that time, Carroll had provided an interesting postscript in the form of a dozen GT-350 convertibles built from restored '66 Mustangs—essentially brand-new cars identical to his original sextet of prototypes. To no one's surprise, they sold quickly despite their $40,000 price tag.

SHELBY AT A GLANCE, 1965-1969					
	1965	1966	1967	1968	1969
Price Range, $			3995-	4117-	4434-
	4547	4600	4195	4594	5027
Weight Range, lbs.			2800-	3000-	3000-
	2800	2800	3000	3300	3200
Wheelbases, in.	108	108	108	108	108
8 Cyl. Engines, hp			290-	250-	290-
	306	306	400	400	400

S tudebaker's 1966 demise was not unexpected. The firm had been through many downturns, rescue attempts, and relapses since the mid-Fifties. By the mid-Sixties, it was too far gone to save.

The troubles can be traced all the way back to the Great Depression, when Studebaker slipped into receivership. After rebounding strongly with the handsome, low-cost 1939 Champion, the company enjoyed record production in the booming late-Forties seller's market by being "first by far with a postwar car." But that was both premature and costly, and Studebaker hung on to the design too long. Its all-new 1953s, which included the first of the now-coveted European-styled "Loewy coupes," might have turned things around, but were hampered by marketing miscalculations, deteriorating workmanship, and a disintegrating dealer body. A desperate 1954 merger with Packard brought problems of its own. By 1958, increasingly unsalable products and fast-falling public confidence had brought Studebaker to the brink of extinction.

A reprieve came with the compact 1959 Lark. Perfectly timed for the market's sudden swing to economy, the Lark gave Studebaker its first profit in five years. But the advent of Big Three compacts and Studebaker's inability to keep the Lark competitive caused sales to slide again after 1960. Studebaker had other products, the sporty Hawk and high-performance Avanti, but these would always be low-volume sideliners. More comeback schemes followed and failed until financial backers gave up.

Predictably, the 1960 Larks were much like the debut '59s save minor trim and a different grille insert (mesh replacing horizontal bars). Wheelbase remained 108.5 inches except on wagons, which continued at 113 and again included four-doors (revived from '58) as well as two-doors. Engines were Studebaker's familiar but aging L-head six and ohv V-8. The former, a 169.6-cubic-inch "stroker," gave 90 horsepower in Deluxe two- and four-door sedans and wagons and the plusher Regal four-door sedan, hardtop coupe, and four-door wagon. Lark's V-8 (which originated in 1951) was a 259 with 180 bhp in standard form or 195 optional. Available in the same models as the six for about $280 more, the V-8 was standard for another 1960 newcomer, a pretty convertible. Prices were bumped up slightly to $2000-$2700. With new Big Three competition, Lark lost some 6600 sales, ending at 126,885. (Unless otherwise noted, figures cited are for U.S./Canadian *model-year* production, excluding exports).

The other Studebaker of these years was the Hawk "family sports car," evolved from the dashing "Loewy coupe." Steadily falling demand had diminished the initial four-model 1956 flock to a single Silver Hawk by 1959. Its 1960 follow-up, now simply Hawk, remained a pillared coupe with 120.5-inch wheelbase, square grille, and outward-curving tailfins (the last added for '57). The main change involved engines, the previous six and 259 V-8 replaced by a 289 V-8 with 210 bhp or, with optional "Power Pack" (four-barrel carburetor and dual exhausts), 225 bhp. Though dated, the 1960 Hawk was a fine value at $2650, and a good performer. Alas, model-year sales dropped by almost half from '59, to 3939, owing to a shortage of dealers and continued advertising emphasis on Lark.

1960 Lark VIII Regal convertible coupe

1960 Lark VIII four-door sedan

1960 Hawk coupe

1961 Lark VI Regal convertible coupe

Ominously, Lark volume fell by more than half for 1961 despite revised outer sheetmetal imparting a slightly squarer look, a new ohv cylinder head that lifted the old six to 112 bhp, and the addition of a V-8 Lark Cruiser. The last, reviving the traditional luxury Studebaker, rode the wagon chassis and boasted a richly upholstered interior with extra rear legroom. Hawk returned with a narrow contrast-color panel beneath its fins and an optional four-speed gearbox. Sales slipped to 3340.

1962 Gran Turismo Hawk hardtop coupe

1963 Daytona four-door wagon

1962 Lark four-door sedan

1963 Avanti sport coupe

1963 Lark Daytona hardtop coupe

Shortly after becoming Studebaker president in early '61, Sherwood Egbert asked Milwaukee-based industrial designer Brooks Stevens to rework both Lark and Hawk within six months. Company styling chief Randall Faurot stepped back, and Stevens conjured up cheap but remarkably effective facelifts for '62. Larks gained elongated rear quarters, large round taillights, a Mercedes-like grille (Studebaker was then the North American Mercedes-Benz distributor), and crisper non-wagon rooflines. Two-door wagons vanished, but there were four new Daytona models—a six and V-8 convertible and hardtop with bucket seats and deluxe trim.

For the '62 Hawk, Stevens resurrected the old "Loewy" hardtop body and applied a square, Thunderbird-style roof, matching deck, rear fenders bereft of fins, and a thrust-forward grille. He also penned a new dash carrying full instrumentation in a large rectangle with outboard ends canted in toward the driver. Renamed Gran Turismo Hawk and offered only with 289s, it was a deft piece of work. Quick, too, the optional 225-bhp V-8 good for 120 mph flat out and a 0-60-mph dash of under 10 seconds. Though heavy, the 289 was strong, with far greater power potential than its modest size implied—as we'd soon see. Hawk sales swelled to nearly 8400 for '62. Total Studebaker volume jumped by over 30,000 units to some 101,400. It would be the only gain of the decade.

There were further Stevens updates for '63. Larks got raked A-pillars and new windshields, revised door-window frames, a finely checked grille insert, and a new dash with round gauges, rocker switches, and a "vanity" glovebox with pop-up mirror. Also new, and quite novel, was the "Wagonaire." Offered in Standard, Regal and Daytona trim, it sported a unique rear-half roof panel that could slide forward for unlimited "head room"—perfect for hauling tall loads. Unfortunately, Wagonaires leaked badly even when closed up, which probably explains why fixed-roof companions were reinstated during the year. Further expanding the line were six and V-8 sedans in stripped Standard and nicer Custom trim, the latter priced between Regal and Daytona.

The '63 GT Hawk displayed a revised grille similar to Lark's, round parking lights (amber, per new federal law), woodgrain dash trim, and pleated-vinyl seats. By midseason, both Lark and Hawk could be ordered with new "Avanti" 289 V-8s: a 240-bhp R1 and a 290-bhp supercharged R2, priced at $210 and $372, respectively. An R2-equipped "Super Hawk" exceeded 140 mph at Bonneville that year; an R2 "Super Lark" did over 132 mph.

Those engines came from the totally unexpected grand-touring coupe that debuted during '62. The most stunning Studebaker in 10 years, the Avanti lived up to its name—"forward" in Italian—brilliantly conceived by Raymond Loewy and beautifully executed by John Ebstein, Robert Andrews, and Tom Kellogg. Because Stevens was fully occupied with "volume" styling, president Egbert had turned to Loewy and Associates for an exotic sporty car that he thought would rejuvenate Studebaker's sagging image—a swoopy four-seater of the sort Loewy had been designing for years.

For this first Studebaker assignment since the '56 Hawks,

1964 Lark Daytona four-door sedan

1964 Lark Daytona hardtop coupe

1964 Gran Turismo Hawk hardtop coupe

1964 Lark Daytona convertible coupe

Loewy secretly gathered his three-man team at a rented house in Palm Springs, California. There they evolved a curvaceous coupe with compound-curve rear window and sharp-edged front fenders swept back to "coke-bottle" flanks and a high "ducktail." There was hardly a straight line anywhere, and the bumpers were little more than thin blades. Headlamps flanked a "grille-less" nose, a large open "mouth" below taking its place. Sloped up and back on the left of the hood was a longitudinal bulge intended to direct driver vision forward, though it mainly added character. Inside, ample padding and a functional, built-in roll bar combined with four slim-section vinyl bucket seats, full instrumentation in a curved cluster, and a center console sprouting large chrome-headed levers for a racy "cockpit" ambience. Completed within a mere six weeks, the Avanti design was approved for production with little change from the team's original quarter-scale model.

As with Chevrolet's first Corvette a decade earlier, fiberglass was chosen for the Avanti bodyshell to minimize both time and tooling costs. There was no time or money for a new chassis, so chief engineer Gene Hardig beefed up a Lark convertible frame with front and rear anti-roll bars, rear radius rods, and the Bendix front-disc power brakes newly optional for Lark and Hawk (the first caliper discs in U.S. production, by the way). Their obvious engine was the 289 V-8, which was heavily revised to become a "Jet Thrust." The basic R1 version employed ¾-race high-lift cam, dual-breaker distributor, four-barrel carb, and dual exhaust. Andy Granatelli's Paxton Products, then part of Studebaker, devised the R2 (an R1 with Paxton blower), plus a trio of bored-out, 304.5-cid extensions: super-

charged R3 with 9.6:1 compression and 335 bhp; naturally aspirated R4 with twin four-barrels, 12:1 compression, and 280 bhp; and the astounding, experimental R5 with twin blowers (one per cylinder bank), magneto ignition, Bendix fuel injection, and an incredible 575 bhp.

The Avanti proved to have very good aerodynamics, though Loewy had just guessed at the shape, Egbert's push for early introduction having precluded wind-tunnel tests. As proof of its prowess, Granatelli broke 29 speed records at Bonneville in late 1962 with an R3 Avanti.

Immediately generating a great deal of excitement, the Avanti promised to pack Studebaker showrooms like nothing else in years. Alas, production was delayed a critical six months by botched bodies from supplier Molded Fiber Glass Co. (which also built Corvette shells), forcing Studebaker to set up its own fiberglass facility. By the time the bugs were worked out, most buyers with advance orders had cancelled and bought Corvettes. As a result, only 3834 Avantis (including exports) were built for '63.

Overall, Studebaker's 1963 volume was well down from '62, skidding to 77,255. Only Lincoln and Imperial ranked lower among major U.S. makes. Egbert, who'd been repeatedly hospitalized, left in November, never to return. (He succumbed to cancer in 1969.) A month later, new president Byers Burlingame announced the closure of Studebaker's historic South Bend plant after last-ditch efforts to obtain financing for future models failed. Operations were consolidated at the firm's Canadian assembly plant in Hamilton, Ontario, where management hoped to return to profitability on 20,000 cars a year, all family compacts. With that, the Avanti and GT Hawk were unceremonious-

1964 Avanti sport coupe

1965 Cruiser four-door sedan

1965 Daytona Sport two-door sedan

1966 Daytona two-door sedan

ly dumped after a token run of little-changed '64 models: just 809 and 1767, respectively (including exports).

Also among the last South Bend Studebakers were the first '64 Larks, all with crisply square new outer body panels, again courtesy of Brooks Stevens. Overall length grew six inches, the grille became a horizontal affair with an eggcrate trapezoid and integral headlights, and a pointy new rear end carried high-set tail/back-up lamps. The stripped Standard was retagged Lark Challenger and priced from $1943, the hallowed Commander name returned to replace Custom/Regal, a four-door Daytona sedan was added, and the Avanti R3 option became available (reducing a Super Lark's 0-60 time to 7.3 seconds). The R3 was also listed for the GT Hawk, which bowed out with "landau" roof styling and optional rear vinyl half-top, plus a smoothed-off rear deck and matte-black dash appliqué. Studebaker sales kept sliding: fewer than 20,000 for calendar '64, about 44,400 for the model year.

The '65 line was pared to just 10 models: six and V-8 Cruiser, two- and four-door Commander sedans, Commander wagon, V-8 Daytona Wagonaire (with and without sliding roof), and a new Daytona pillared sport coupe. Styling was unchanged. Closing South Bend ended Studebaker engine production, so management ultimately settled on Chevrolet substitutes: 120-bhp 194 six and the excellent 283 small-block V-8 in 195-bhp tune.

Hamilton almost managed 20,000 cars for '65, but without facilities for developing replacement models, Studebaker had little future as an automaker. Besides, financing was all but gone. The 1966 models thus became the last Studebakers, basically warmed-over '65s with dual-beam headlights (replacing quads), a new four-slot grille, and air-extractor vents inboard of smaller taillights. Only 8947 were built.

Studebaker itself did not die, becoming a diversified investment and real-estate company, while the svelte Avanti would live on in modified form until the early Nineties. Even the once-planned "four-door Avanti" saw the light of day. Built by the same Avanti Automotive Corp. at a modern factory in Youngstown, Ohio, it was tooled from Studebaker's own prototype body for the suggested '66 passenger-car line, left behind in the crumbling remains of the giant South Bend plant. Sadly, Loewy died before its early-1990 introduction, but he would have been pleased that two of his greatest works were so long produced—and appreciated.

STUDEBAKER AT A GLANCE, 1960-1966							
	1960	1961	1962	1963	1964	1965	1966
Price Range, $	1976-2756	1935-2689	1935-3080	1935-4445	1943-4445	2125-2890	2060-2695
Weight Range, lbs.	2588-3315	2661-3315	2655-3305	2650-3490	2660-3555	2695-3505	2695-3501
Wheelbases, in.	108.5-120.5	108.5-120.5	109-120.5	109-120.5	109-120.5	109-113	109-113
6 Cyl. Engines, hp		90	112	112	112	120	120-140
8 Cyl. Engines, hp	180-225	180-225	180-225	180-290	180-335	195	195

PRODUCTION CHARTS

Automotive production figures can be confusing, because car makers and industry observers sometimes discuss production in terms of model years and calendar years. The two are not the same; each firm builds cars of two different model years between January 1 and December 31 of a single calendar year.

The following chart lists production figures for model years rather than calendar years unless otherwise specified. (Most of the figures discussed in the text of *Cars of the '60s* are calendar-year figures.)

	1960	1961	1962	1963	1964	1965	1966	1967	1968	1969
AMC										
Ambassador							71,692	62,615	54,641	75,741
AMX									6,725	8,293
Javelin									56,462	40,675
Marlin							4,547	2,545		
Rebel									69,607	48,397
BUICK										
Special		74,185	110,870	106,449	98,762	101,601	103,097	86,041	49,475	35,648
Skylark		12,683	42,973	42,321	85,870	133,368	106,217	107,292	178,025	152,695
LeSabre	152,082	113,230	127,198	171,183	135,163	144,996	142,399	155,190	179,748	197,866
Invicta	45,411	28,733	56,017	3,495						
Wildcat				35,725	82,245	98,787	68,584	70,881	69,969	67,453
Riviera				40,000	37,658	34,586	45,348	42,799	49,284	52,872
Electra	56,314	47,923	62,468	58,665	68,792	86,807	88,225	100,304	125,362	158,618
CADILLAC										
Series 62	70,842	62,426	70,277	64,298	52,979					
Calais						34,211	28,680	21,830	18,190	12,425
De Ville	53,389	55,174	55,653	79,049	92,496	123,080	142,190	139,807	164,472	163,048
Eldorado	2,443	1,450	1,450	1,825	1,870	2,125	2,250	17,930	24,528	23,333
60 Special	11,800	15,500	13,350	14,000	14,550	18,100	19,075	16,300	18,600	19,845
Series 75	1,550	1,625	1,600	1,475	1,425	1,250	2,017	1,800	1,800	2,036
Comm. Chassis	2,160	2,204	2,280	2,527	2,639	2,669	2,463	2,333	2,413	2,550
CHECKER ■	6,980	5,683	8,173	7,050	6,310	6,136	5,761	5,822	5,477	5,417
CHEVROLET ▲										
Biscayne	287,700	204,000	166,000	186,500	173,900	145,300	122,400	92,800	82,100	68,700
Bel Air	381,500	330,000	365,500	354,100	318,100	271,400	236,600	179,700	152,200	155,700
Impala	511,900	491,000	704,900	832,600	889,600	803,400	654,900	575,600	710,900	777,000
Wagon	212,700	(inc, above)	187,600	198,500	192,800	184,400	185,500	155,100	175,600	(inc, above)
Chevy II			326,600	375,600	191,700	122,100	163,300	106,500	201,000	270,000
Chevelle					328,400	344,100	412,000	396,100	422,900	439,600
Impala SS					243,100	119,300	74,000			
Caprice							181,000	124,500	115,500	166,900
Camaro								220,900	235,100	243,100
CHEV. CORVAIR										
500	62,311	41,200	16,245	16,680	22,968	54,307	32,824	12,216	7,206	2,762
700	175,770	97,185	57,558	33,062	16,295					
Monza	11,926	143,690	209,560	185,730	140,781	152,557	60,447	15,037	8,193	3,238
Monza Spyder			9,468	19,099	11,411					
Corsa						28,654	10,472			
CHEV. CORVETTE										
Convertible	10,261	10,939	14,531	10,919	13,925	15,376	17,762	14,436	18,630	16,608
Coupe				10,594	8,304	8,186	9,958	8,504	9,936	22,154

■ *(Calendar year, includes taxicabs)*
▲ *(Chevrolet production rounded to nearest 100)*

	1960	1961	1962	1963	1964	1965	1966	1967	1968	1969
CHRYSLER										
Windsor	41,158	17,336								
Saratoga	15,525									
Newport		57,102	83,120	75,972	85,183	125,795	167,711	157,371	182,099	156,836
"300"			25,020	24,665	25,318	27,678	49,597	21,888	34,621	32,472
New Yorker	19,390	20,399	20,223	27,960	31,044	49,871	47,579	39,457	48,143	46,947
300F to 300L	1,212	1,617	558	400	3,647	2,845				
Town & Country □										24,516
DESOTO										
Fireflite	14,484									
Adventurer	11,597									
(standard)		3,034								
DODGE (U.S. & CANADA)										
Lancer		74,774	64,271							
Dart	323,168	180,561	146,360	153,922	192,673	209,376	176,027	154,495	171,772	197,685
Matador	27,908									
330/440				148,100	188,403					
880			17,505	28,266	31,760	44,496				
Polara	16,728	14,032	12,268	7,256	88,585	109,811	107,832	76,464	106,687	91,721
Coronet						209,392	250,842	183,802	220,831	203,425
Monaco						13,096	60,613	40,462	41,980	38,566
Charger							37,344	15,788	96,108	89,700
EDSEL										
Ranger	2,571									
Villager	275									
FORD										
Falcon	435,676	474,241	414,282	328,399	300,770	213,601	182,669	64,335	131,389	96,016
Custom/300/500	874	352		70,152	188,770	236,757	243,775	160,930	122,846	114,438
Fairlane	204,793	163,477	79,606	97,444	47,114	52,974	83,431	65,499	102,592	123,808
Fairlane 500	244,275	141,385	217,510	246,443	230,472	170,980	233,643	173,189	114,425	114,049
Galaxie/500XL	289,268	349,665	170,524	112,754					56,114	61,959
Galaxie 500			404,600	535,256	593,533	457,129	495,904	426,941	339,262	311,388
station wagon	171,824	136,619	129,654	127,130	140,929	177,664	195,153	178,751	208,318	238,523
LTD (Galaxie model, 1965-66)						105,729	101,096	110,505	138,752	288,442
Torino (Fairlane model) △									157,310	129,058
FORD MUSTANG										
fastback						77,079	35,698	71,042	42,581	61,980
hardtop						501,965	499,751	356,271	249,447	128,458
convertible						101,945	72,119	44,808	25,376	14,746

□ *(from 1960 through 1968: included under individual series above)*
△ Note: *Falcon, Fairlane & Torino include wagons: Falcon Econoline & Club Wagon not included*

1964½ Chrysler 300 hardtop coupe

1960 Dodge Polara hardtop sedan

	1960	1961	1962	1963	1964	1965	1966	1967	1968	1969
Mach I										72,458
Grande										22,182
FORD THUNDERBIRD										
hardtop	80,983	62,535	68,127	42,806	60,552	42,652	29,022	15,567	9,977	5,913
convertible	11,860	10,516	8,457	5,913	9,198	6,846	5,049			
Sports Roadster			1,427	455						
Landau, 2 dr.				14,139	22,715	25,474	35,105	37,422	33,029	27,664
Landau, 4 dr.								24,967	21,925	15,695
IMPERIAL										
Custom/Standard	7,786	5,018	4,413	4,013				2,193	1,887	
Crown	8,226	6,205	8,475	8,558	20,336	16,235	11,864	13,227	12,622	2,684
Le Baron	1,691	1,026	1,449	1,537	2,949	2,164	1,878	2,194	1,852	19,393
Crown Imperial	16	9	0	13	10	10	10			
Le Baron limousine							estimated:	6	6	6
LINCOLN										
standard	7,160									
Premiere	6,574									
Continental sedan		22,307	27,849	28,095	32,969	36,824	35,809	32,331	29,719	29,258
Continental convert.		2,857	3,212	3,138	3,328	3,356	3,180	2,276		
Continental coupe							15,766	11,060	9,415	9,032
Mark V	11,086									
Mark III									7,770	23,088
MERCURY										
Comet & Montego	116,331	197,263	165,305	134,623	189,936	165,052	170,426	81,133	123,113	117,421
Meteor/S-55			53,122	69,052	50,775		3,585			
Monterey	102,539	50,128	89,024	107,072	42,587	80,373	65,688	49,398	57,014	53,065
Montclair	19,814				32,963	45,546	38,913	19,922	14,760	
Park Lane	10,287				19,611	32,405	38,800	20,476	14,803	
station wagon ▲	22,360	16,838	17,985	13,976	15,181	23,375	25,741	26,588	29,867	33,368
Cougar								150,893	113,726	100,069
Marquis								6,510	3,965	43,436
Brougham									5,691	37,962
Marauder										14,666
METROPOLITAN										
1500 ○	13,103	853	412							
OLDSMOBILE										
F-85/Cutlass		76,394	94,568	118,811	177,618	212,870	229,573	251,461	275,128	239,289
Dynamic 88	189,864	138,380	188,737	199,315	167,674	119,497	95,834			
Super 88	97,913	53,164	58,147	62,770	37,514					

▲ *(Note: "station wagon" covers full-size wagons only.)*
○ *(Shipments from U.K.)*

1966 Ford Mustang GT convertible coupe

1962 Lincoln Continental convertible sedan

	1960	1961	1962	1963	1964	1965	1966	1967	1968	1969
Jetstar/Delmont 88					78,589	61,989	30,247	108,356	121,418	
Delta 88						90,467	88,626	88,096	102,505	252,087
Ninety Eight	59,364	43,012	64,154	70,308	68,554	92,406	88,494	76,539	92,072	116,783
Starfire		7,600	41,988	25,549	16,163	15,260	13,019			
Toronado							40,963	21,790	26,521	28,520
PLYMOUTH	483,969	356,257	339,527	488,448	551,633	728,228	687,514	638,075	790,239	751,134
PONTIAC										
Tempest		100,783	143,193	131,490	226,577	231,731	262,152	184,738	258,722	215,628
GTO						32,450	75,352	96,946	81,722	87,684	72,287
Catalina	210,934	113,354	204,654	234,549	257,768	271,058	254,310	240,750	276,182	246,596
Ventura	56,277	27,209								
Starchief/Executive	43,691	29,581	41,642	40,757	37,653	31,315	45,212	46,987	44,635	39,061
Bonneville	85,227	69,323	101,753	109,539	120,259	134,020	135,401	102,996	104,436	96,315
Firebird								82,560	107,112	87,708
Grand Prix			30,195	72,959	63,810	57,881	36,757	42,981	31,711	112,486
RAMBLER										
(Total registrations)	422,273	370,685	423,104	428,346	379,412	324,669	265,712	237,785	259,346	239,937
SHELBY										
GT-350						562	2,378	1,175	1,648	1,279
GT-500								2,050	1,557	1,871
GT-500KR									1,246	
STUDEBAKER										
2-dr. sedan	30,453	13,275	17,636	15,726	5,485	7,372	2,321			
4-dr. sedan	48,382	28,670	41,894	30,795	15,908	10,239	5,686			
2-dr. hardtop	6,867	3,211	7,888	3,259	1,734					
2-dr. wagon	4,833	2,166								
4-dr. wagon	17,902	6,552	9,687	10,487	3,702	1,824	440			
convertible	8,306	1,898	2,599	773	411					
Hawk	3,719	3,117	7,842	3,649	1,484					
Avanti				3,744	795					
taxi & chassis	3	824	1,772	1,121	450					

1961 Pontiac Catalina Sport two-door sedan

1960 Studebaker Lark VI four-door wagon